IMAGES
of America

GREENBELT

IMAGES
of America

GREENBELT

Jill Parsons St. John and
Megan Searing Young on behalf of
the Friends of the Greenbelt Museum

ARCADIA
PUBLISHING

Published by Arcadia Publishing
Charleston, South Carolina

Printed in the United States of America

Library of Congress Control Number: 2011930645

For all general information, please contact Arcadia Publishing:
Telephone 843-853-2070
Fax 843-853-0044
E-mail sales@arcadiapublishing.com
For customer service and orders:
Toll-Free 1-888-313-2665

Visit us on the Internet at www.arcadiapublishing.com

CONTENTS

ACKNOWLEDGMENTS

This book was produced as a project of the 75th anniversary of Greenbelt, Maryland, and was made possible by the Greenbelt City Council and the Friends of the Greenbelt Museum.

First, we would like to thank the dedicated, forward-thinking, and determined group of people who envisioned and founded the Greenbelt Museum on the occasion of the city's 50th anniversary in 1987. They are Barbara Havekost, Sandy Lange, Dorothy Lauber, Mary Linstrom, Janie Mutschler, Christina O'Boyle, Martha Sinden, Sally Sims Stokes, Dorothy Sucher, Alan Virta, Don Volk, Linda Warner, and Dorothy White. Their perseverance and hard work paved the way for our curatorial predecessors, Ann Denkler and Katie Scott Childress, both of whom also shaped the Greenbelt Museum and further contributed to the preservation of Greenbelt's history. In addition, we are grateful to Greenbelt's city council, city staff, the nonprofit Friends of the Greenbelt Museum, and the many dedicated museum volunteers who all make the Greenbelt Museum viable and support the collection, preservation, and celebration of Greenbelt's unique history.

There are many Greenbelt families, too numerous to mention here, who have been exceedingly generous over the years with their memories, photographs, artifacts, and diaries—to them the museum is extremely grateful. For this project, we would like to thank the following families and individuals who contributed photographs and information: Brenda Cooley, Ray Frank, Marion Benson Hastings, Eugenia Horstmann, Bob Sommers, John Henry Jones, the Maffays, Richard Rosenzweig, and Lee and Bonnie Shields. These are only a few of the people who have shared generously with the museum; there are many more on the pages of this book. We would also like to thank the staff of the *Greenbelt News Review*, particularly Mary Lou Williamson and Eileen Farnham, for allowing us access to their archives.

We would also like to thank the many advisors, editors, and scholars who have helped in the process of putting this book together: Isabelle Gournay, Mary Corbin Sies, Michael McLaughlin, David Moran, Stephen Oetken, Sheila Maffay-Tuthill, Jennifer Ruffner, and especially Kathy Karlson. Their insights and advice throughout this process were invaluable. In addition, we would like to thank our families, Bill and Sarah Parsons; Aaron, Sylvia, and Wilson St. John; Daniel and Mary Lou Searing; and Kelly, Maeve, and Edina Young.

INTRODUCTION

Greenbelt, Maryland, is a planned community designed and built by the federal government in the late 1930s. From its comprehensive plan and careful construction to its lasting commitment to cooperative living, the community is an example of the innovation that can sometimes result from desperation. As Americans struggled under the weight of the Great Depression, Franklin Delano Roosevelt was elected president. He established the New Deal, a series of agencies and programs to help Americans recover. One of those agencies was the Resettlement Administration, created in 1935 and headed by Rexford Guy Tugwell, an economist and one of Roosevelt's trusted advisors. Some of the agency's initiatives were to resettle people from failing farms, arid land, and overcrowded, unhealthy cities. Tugwell dreamed of building entirely new communities called "greenbelt towns" on the outskirts of major metropolitan areas encircled by belts of green space, combining the best of country and city living. Greenbelt was the first of three green towns that were built. It was a relief project, so its construction put many people to work. It also provided much needed low-income housing for families, which was difficult to find in the Washington, DC, area. Despite being built by both African American and white workers, Greenbelt was originally only open to white families, as it was a segregated community. In addition, Greenbelt's planners intended that it would be a model of modern town planning, which private industry would replicate.

While the government had been experimenting with building low-income housing for several years, Tugwell's vision was specifically based on the garden city concept first envisioned by Ebenezer Howard in 1898. Howard, in response to the increasing industrialization and unhealthful living conditions of urban areas in the United Kingdom in the late 19th century, proposed the construction of smaller towns on the outskirts of cities surrounded by green space with areas for people to live, work, and play. Beyond the belt of green space, farmers would grow crops that could easily be sold to the nearby townspeople. Howard's ideas were known in the United States and influenced urban planners such as Clarence Stein, who was a consultant on the Greenbelt project. Stein, along with Henry Wright, designed Radburn, New Jersey, in 1929, which is based on garden city principles and includes superblocks, underpasses, pedestrian walkways, and carefully designed housing, all features that would eventually be included in Greenbelt's design as well.

Unlike typical American towns that evolve over time as a result of economic factors and population demand, Greenbelt was carefully created from scratch on worn-out farmland 14 miles outside of Washington, DC. A forward-thinking group of administrators, planners, and architects intended to demonstrate that planned development was far superior to haphazard development and that the physical design of a community could positively influence the lives of its residents. Greenbelt's innovative design, based on both the garden cities of England and Radburn, New Jersey, features residential superblocks four to five times the size of a standard city block and homes with an unusual orientation. Service entries, normally associated with back-of-the-house activities such as trash collection and laundry, actually faced the street, and the garden side or main entries faced the interior of the block, which was shared green space. This configuration provided access to walking paths that wound through the blocks and under roads via underpasses, connecting the homes to numerous parks and playgrounds as well as to a town center. Greenbelt is one of three completed federal green towns, with the others being Greendale, Wisconsin, and Greenhills, Ohio. A fourth, planned for New Jersey, was never built. In 1997, Greenbelt's innovative plan became a National Historic Landmark.

The architecture of the town also reflects the planners' forward-thinking ideas. The town's original school, now a thriving community center, is one of the best-known examples of municipal Art Deco architecture in the region. It features bas-reliefs by Works Progress Administration (WPA) sculptor Lenore Thomas, whose statue *The Mother and Child* also graces the town center. The center of town, which featured cooperative businesses run by town residents, still boasts a cinema complete with Art Deco marquee (restored in 2000), a cooperative grocery store, and a variety of small shops and services. In addition to planning the environment, the government worked initially to facilitate the cooperative businesses and volunteer organizations. Residents got involved immediately by forming numerous committees, churches, groups, sports teams, and organizations, one of which eventually took over the cooperatives. The town is also famous for its recreational facilities. The original swimming pool, ball fields, tennis courts, man-made lake, and shared green spaces have long been enjoyed and celebrated by residents and people from nearby towns.

World War II and the decades that followed brought many changes to Greenbelt, most notably 1,000 more dwellings. Initially envisioned to be temporary housing that would be torn down at the end of the war, the homes are still being used today. The newly expanded Greenbelt weathered Word War II with scrap metal drives, black-out drills, and fundraising dances. Then, in 1952, the federal government sold the green towns, and Greenbelt was purchased by residents who formed what was initially a veterans housing cooperative, now called Greenbelt Homes, Inc. As the Washington metropolitan region grew, more housing was built in the areas around the historic section of Greenbelt. In addition to the city's physical beauty, its residents, both old and new, continue to be one of its greatest resources. Though somewhat subdivided by major roads and highways, citizens of Greenbelt are working to build an inclusive community and share the city's history not just with their neighbors but with the nation in general. As Greenbelt plans to celebrate its 75th anniversary, many are looking toward the community's future and are discussing issues such as stainability, green building, and smart growth. It remains to be seen what new ideas will grow from this unique American city, which rightfully takes its place not just in local history but national history as well.

One

PLANNING A GREENBELT TOWN

Roosevelt created the Resettlement Administration (RA) in the spring of 1935 and appointed Rexford Guy Tugwell as its head. Tugwell assembled a team of advisors, including housing experts, architects, and planners, to help envision the housing projects that the RA would undertake. By the end of the year, planning for the greenbelt towns had begun. John Lansill was appointed director of the Suburban Resettlement Division and was the overseer of all of the greenbelt towns. Wallace Richards was the executive officer in charge of Maryland Project No. 1, as Greenbelt was first known. Greenbelt's chief town planner was Hale Walker. Reginald J. Wadsworth and Douglas D. Ellington were the architects. Additional artists, photographers, draftsmen, and mapmakers were tasked with creating images, posters, renderings, blueprints, and plans that would promote the RA projects and allow them to take shape. According to a 1936 RA promotional booklet, "A greenbelt town is simply a community built on raw land, in which every acre is put to its best use, and in which the traditional dividing lines between town and country are broken down. To the city worker, it offers a home in healthful country surroundings, yet within easy reach of his job. To the small farmer living in the greenbelt area, it offers better facilities and a steady market within a few hundred yards of his own fields. For both of them, it combines the conveniences and cultural opportunities of a city with many advantages of life on the land."

Greenbelt's planners also warned that if the suburbs were not planned with the efficient use of land and a careful blend of residential, commercial, and green spaces, the result would be suburban sprawl and chaotic development. Budgetary and political concerns, as well as litigation, resulted in only three towns being built: Greenbelt, Maryland; Greendale, Wisconsin; and Greenhills, Ohio. The fourth, Greenbrook, New Jersey, was never completed. The towns were not widely duplicated as the country was headed towards World War II in the next decade, but urban planners and academics have long studied them. Elements of their design can be seen in places like Columbia, Maryland, and Reston, Virginia.

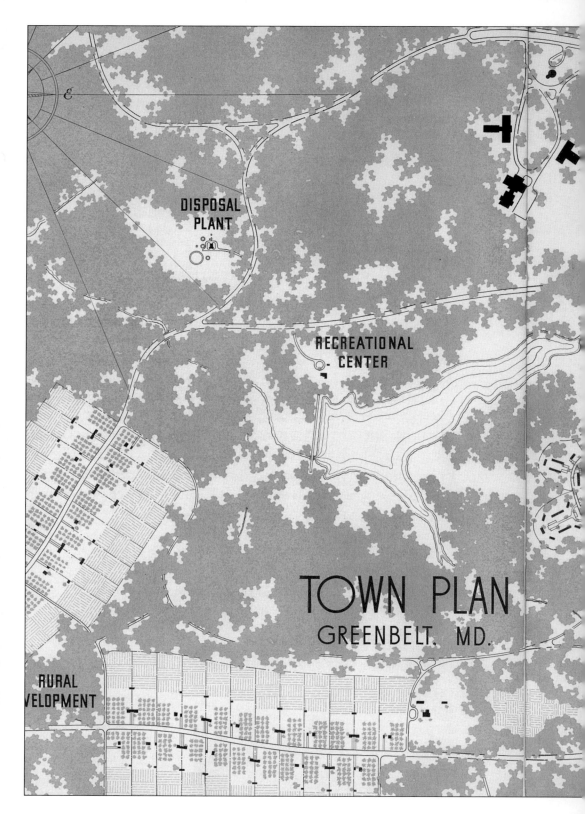

DISPOSAL
PLANT

RECREATIONAL
CENTER

TOWN PLAN
GREENBELT, MD.

RURAL
VELOPMENT

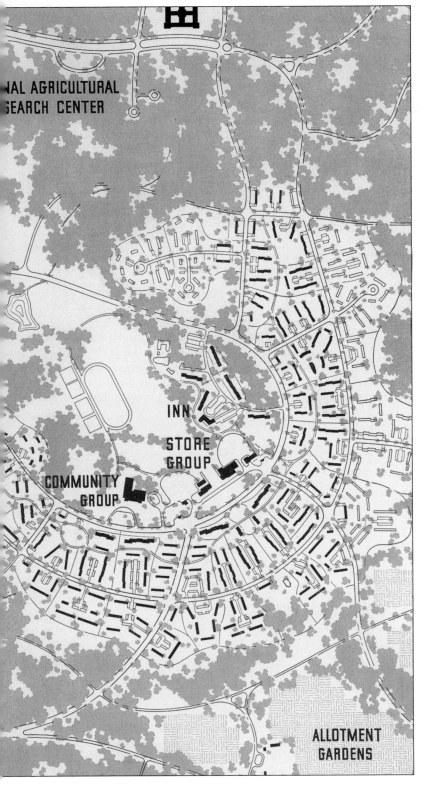

NAL AGRICULTURAL
SEARCH CENTER

INN

STORE
GROUP

COMMUNITY
GROUP

ALLOTMENT
GARDENS

The Resettlement Administration (RA) published a promotional booklet in 1936 entitled "Greenbelt Towns." The text, images, graphs, photographs, and maps, such as this one, included in the booklet not only explained the greenbelt town concept but also attempted to justify the Suburban Resettlement Division's expenditures. Unlike typical American towns that evolved over time, Greenbelt was entirely mapped before construction began. The RA acquired a total of 12,189 acres for the project, including areas for housing, parks, allotment gardens, small farms, and areas set aside for expansion. This map designates space for rural development, which may have been where planners hoped to establish the Rossville Rural Development, an area to be farmed by African American families. This portion of the plan was dropped early on, however, as it was too controversial, and the small farms were never built. Had they been established, they would have supplied the residents with locally grown food, in keeping with the original idea of a garden city. (Courtesy Greenbelt Museum.)

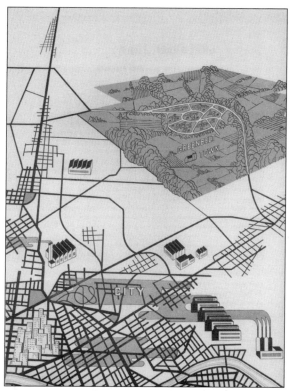

This page from the RA's booklet dramatically illustrates how green towns would be situated as satellite communities on the outskirts of crowded, dense city streets. In selecting sites for the towns, the Suburban Resettlement Division studied 100 different urban areas. It looked for steady growth, diversity of industry, good wage levels, what it referred to as "enlightened labor policies," and a shortage of housing. (Courtesy Greenbelt Museum.)

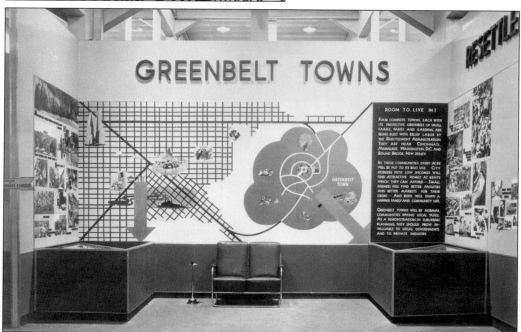

The RA was actively engaged in promoting itself and the work it was doing. It set up exhibits at several of the expositions in the 1930s, including the one pictured above at the Great Lakes Exposition, held in Cleveland, Ohio, in the summers of 1936 and 1937. Many of the same graphics and photographs appear in the RA booklet. (Courtesy Library of Congress.)

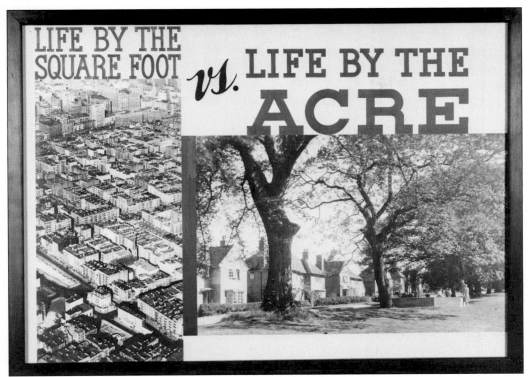

The RA also employed artists to create posters to promote its ideals. This image invites the viewer to compare "life by the square foot versus life by the acre" and contrasts block after block of monotonous dense city buildings with the bucolic tree-lined streets of a planned community. (Courtesy Library of Congress.)

This RA poster is a stark reminder of the living conditions of children in city slums. The green towns were offered as a safe, healthful alternative to life in the overcrowded city, particularly for children. Many historians believe that the green towns were planned largely with children in mind. Greenbelt's original plan, for instance, included three large playgrounds and 13 smaller ones throughout the community. (Courtesy Library of Congress.)

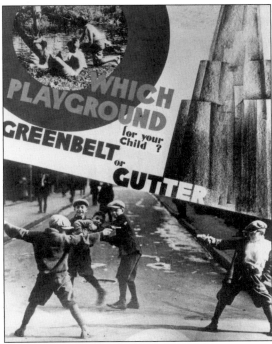

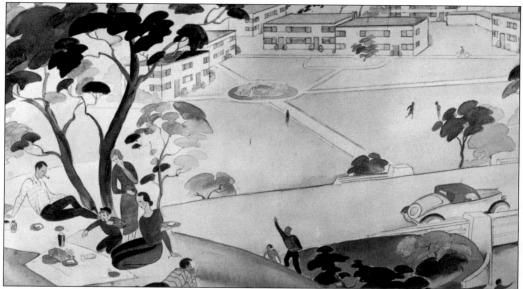

Aurelieus Battaglia was one of the artists employed by the federal government to envision what the green towns would eventually look like. He titled the watercolor above *Utopia*. Born in Washington, DC, in 1910, Battaglia graduated from the Corcoran School of Art and created several works that captured RA ideals. The poster below can also be attributed to Battaglia and graphically highlights one advantage of a green town: a ready market for the local farmers, who farm the land that partially comprises the belt of green space surrounding the town. Following his work for the federal government, Battaglia travelled to California and was employed by the Walt Disney Studios, where he worked on such films as *Dumbo* and *Pinocchio* from 1937 to 1941. (Above, courtesy Greenbelt Museum; below, courtesy Library of Congress.)

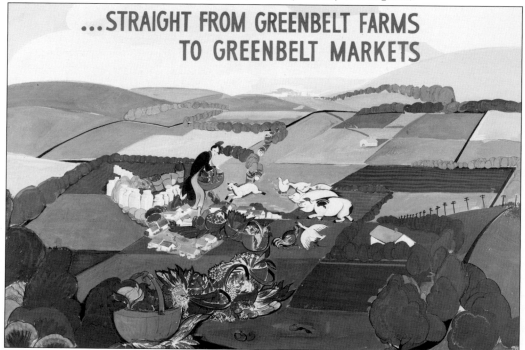

Underpasses, as depicted in this RA rendering, were an integral part of Greenbelt's plan and would allow town residents, both young and old, to cross under streets safely. The five underpasses planned for Greenbelt allowed for separation of vehicular and pedestrian traffic. Underpasses are one of the iconic elements of Greenbelt's design and one of the planning features borrowed from Radburn, New Jersey. (Courtesy Library of Congress.)

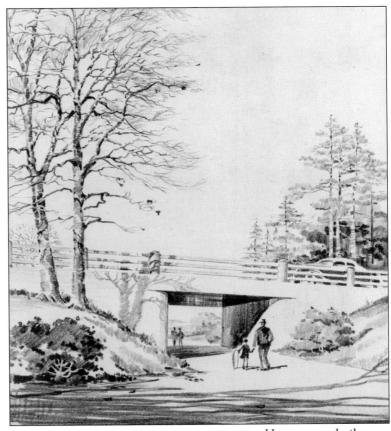

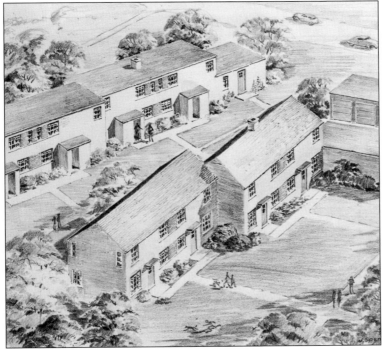

Houses were built in rows of two, four, six, or eight units and organized into courts. Homes did not have traditional front and back doors but instead had garden-side entrances that led to the pathways through the town and service-side entrances that provided access to roads or garages. Activities related to household function took place on the service side: milk and mail were delivered, laundry was hung, and an outdoor closet contained trash cans. (Courtesy Library of Congress.)

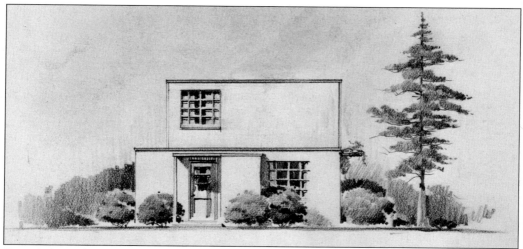

Greenbelt's architects, Douglas D. Ellington and Reginald J. Wadsworth, took cues from a variety of architectural styles, including European Modernist movements. The flat roofs, angular porches, and casement windows featured in this architectural rendering reveal these influences. Primarily two types of houses were built in Greenbelt: cinder block units with flat roofs like this model and wood-frame, brick-veneer homes with peaked slate roofs. (Courtesy Library of Congress.)

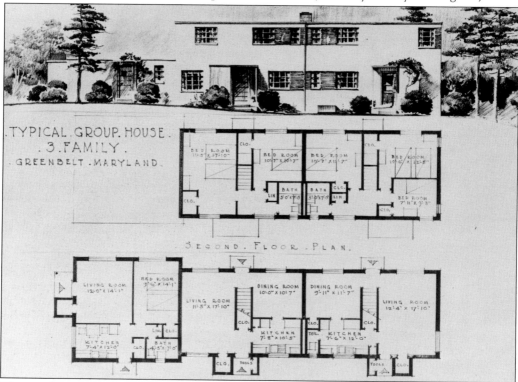

This rendering of housing units includes detailed floor plans. Most units were approximately 17 feet wide, 23 feet deep, and two stories high, though there were some three-story units. Nearly every room had a window, and there was no wasted space. The unit to the left was referred to as a "honeymoon cottage," as those residents assigned to these smaller spaces were often young, married couples who had not yet had children. (Courtesy Library of Congress.)

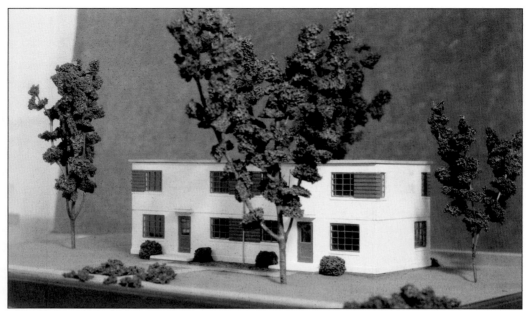

Harry Falls was a draftsman and model maker who, along with young architect Gordon Herr, was employed by the RA to create small three-dimensional models of Greenbelt's topography, homes, and commercial buildings. In a 1987 oral history, he describes how they made the trees from twisted wire and painted sponges. Falls also became a resident of Greenbelt, living first in one of the original units, then in one of the freestanding experimental Parkbelt homes built in Greenbelt by General Houses, Inc., of Chicago. Falls went on to have a long career in many aspects of housing but said that he believed Greenbelt is "the finest example of town planning in the world." (Both, courtesy Library of Congress.)

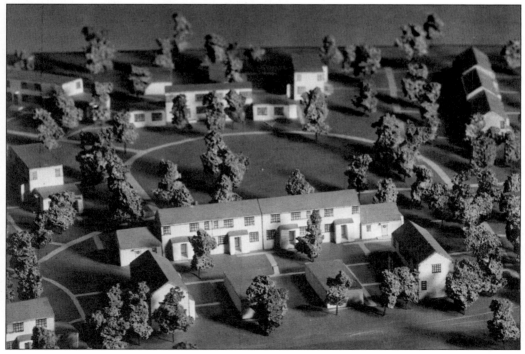

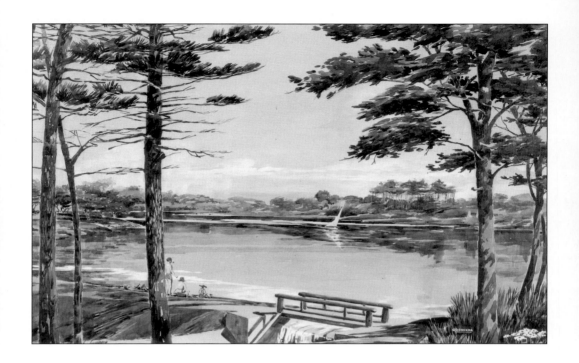

Greenbelt Lake was man-made on low-lying land in the eastern portion of the town plan. The original plans for the lake included a bathhouse and boathouse. The boathouse was to include a dock with a boat rental and launch, sand beach, and changing facilities for bathers. The federal government never built the boathouse or other structures in the original plans due to budgetary concerns. (Above, courtesy Library of Congress; below, courtesy Greenbelt Museum.)

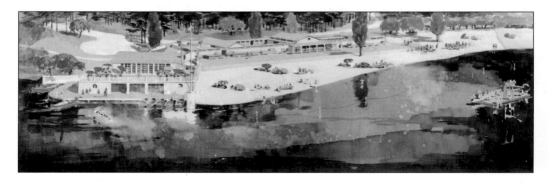

Rexford Guy Tugwell, in his white suit, and John Lansill visited the Greenbelt site in July 1936. Tugwell persuaded FDR to build the three green towns, a controversial idea that many strongly criticized. Greenbelt was often called "Tugwell's Folly," or "Tugwelltown." John Lansill, a friend of Tugwell's from their days together at Wharton Business School, headed the Suburban Resettlement Division, the part of the RA that oversaw construction of the green towns. (Courtesy Library of Congress.)

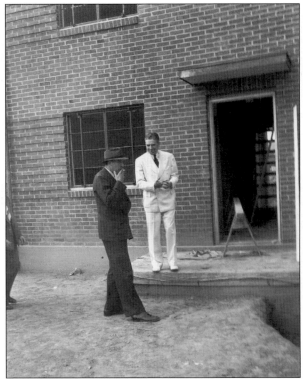

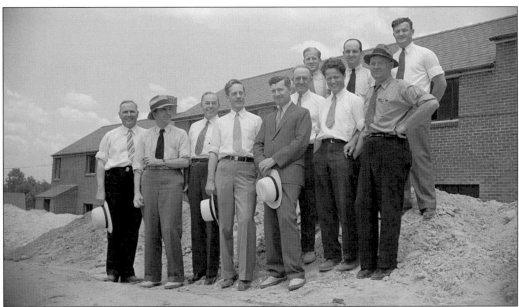

RA officials gathered at the Greenbelt site in July 1936. Wallace Richards, second from the right in the second row, was the executive officer in charge of the Greenbelt project. According to John Lansill, head of the Suburban Resettlement Division, the various green town projects "included the best available talent in the fields of town and site planning, architecture, structural, mechanical and utility engineering, and landscape design. Many were nationally, even internationally known." (Courtesy Library of Congress, photograph by Carl Mydans.)

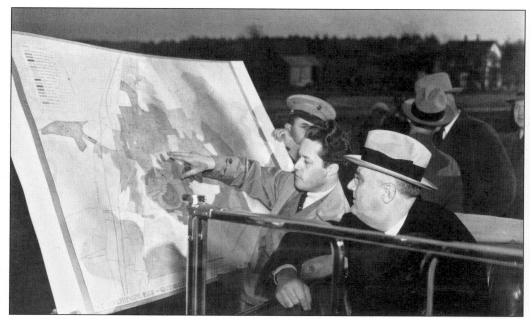

Pres. Franklin D. Roosevelt visited Greenbelt in November 1936 and is shown here reviewing construction plans with Wallace Richards. Roosevelt was quoted in the *Washington Post* as having said during his visit, "Though I have seen the blueprints of Greenbelt, the sight of the project exceeds anything I dreamed of. I wish everyone in the country could see it. . . . The project is an achievement that ought to be copied in every city in the nation." Large crowds gathered to greet the president. Other shots show camera crews positioned on the tops of buildings, shooting footage that would be shown as newsreels in movie theaters. (Both, courtesy Library of Congress.)

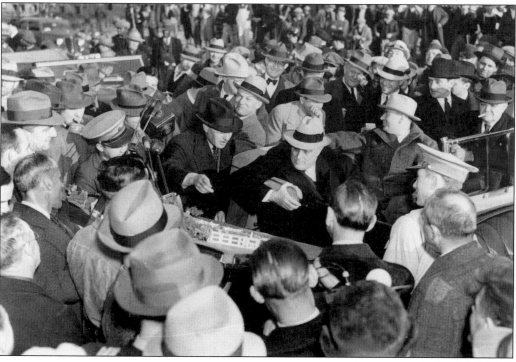

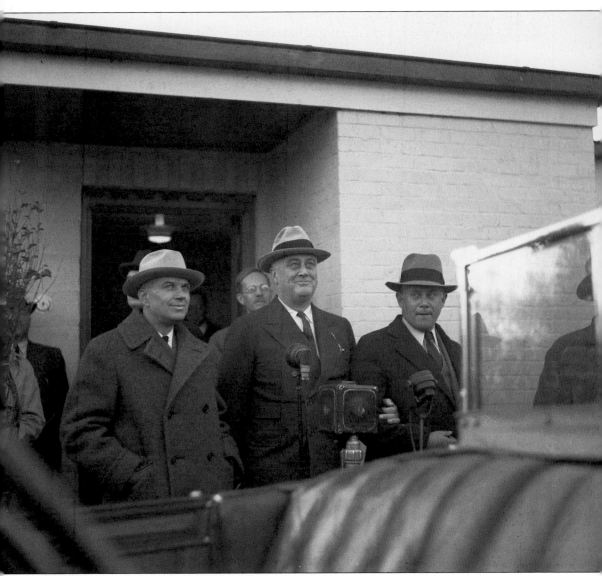

FDR also toured a model home in November 1936 and was photographed standing with Tugwell (left) at his side. According to a *Washington Post* article, the trip had been delayed for several months because of criticism of Tugwell, who was often targeted by those critical of Roosevelt's policies. Tugwell would leave his position as head of the RA at the end of the year, and in 1937, the RA would be absorbed by the Farm Security Administration. (Courtesy Library of Congress, photograph by Arthur Rothstein.)

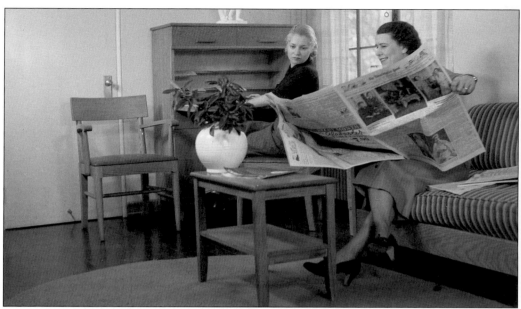

These photographs show a model home on display to the public in the fall of 1936. Furniture was designed specifically for Greenbelt homes by the RA's Special Skills Division. Pieces had multiple uses and were scaled to fit the modest interiors. They were produced by various furniture companies and made available at reasonable prices. They could be added onto residents' monthly rent and paid for over time. According to *House Beautiful* (1937), "On the basis of information about members of the family which would live there, the architect, decorator and designer visualized where they would sleep, study, play and work. They figured out how many chairs, tables, bureaus, desks, bookcases and beds they would need and in what rooms they should be placed. The house, furnishings and interior decoration were then designed to fit." Although the staged photograph below features a dog, pets were not allowed in early Greenbelt. (Both, courtesy Library of Congress, photographs by Arthur Rothstein.)

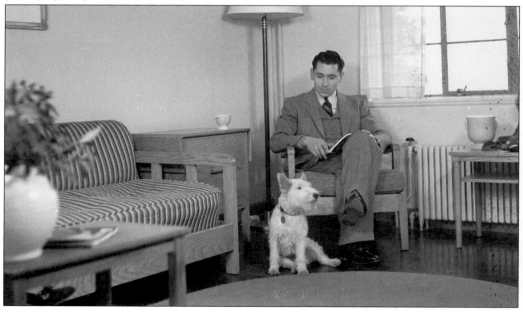

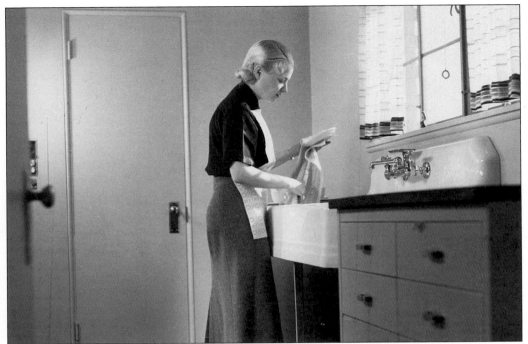

Planners designed the kitchens with as much care as the rest of the homes and incorporated modern kitchen designs of the 1930s. Each unit had an electric stove and refrigerator, large double sink, built-in cabinets, overhead lighting, and a window for proper ventilation. Floors throughout the first floor of the houses were black tile, though some units featured wood floors on the upper level. The floors would prove unpopular. One early resident, Dorothy Harris, remembers, "But the floors. They were the biggest mistake made in the construction of Greenbelt. Ugly black tile, they would not stay shiny no matter what we did. We would clean and wax them, and the first time someone walked across the floor, they would either leave tracks or scratch the tile." Bedrooms were carefully planned as well, and master bedrooms were often situated on the garden side of the house, with children's bedrooms overlooking the service side. (Both, courtesy Greenbelt Museum, photographs by Arthur Rothstein.)

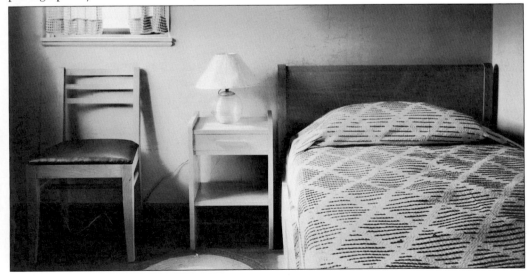

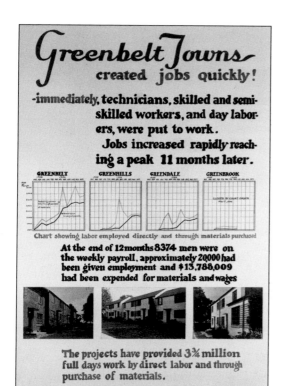

Greenbelt Towns
created jobs quickly!

-immediately, technicians, skilled and semi-skilled workers, and day laborers, were put to work.

Jobs increased rapidly reaching a peak 11 months later.

GREENBELT	GREENHILLS	GREENDALE	GREENBROOK

Chart showing labor employed directly and through materials purchased

At the end of 12 months 8374 men were on the weekly payroll, approximately 20,000 had been given employment and $13,788,009 had been expended for materials and wages

The projects have provided 3¾ million full days work by direct labor and through purchase of materials.

This 1936 poster justified the work of the RA's Suburban Resettlement program. Though four towns were planned, only three were actually built. The fourth, Greenbrook, was to be constructed near New Brunswick, New Jersey, and featured Henry Wright as its chief architect. It was suspended, then closed altogether, because of litigation brought by local citizens who asserted that the Emergency Relief Act of 1935, which funded the RA, was unconstitutional. They also feared loss of tax revenue since the land would be government owned. (Courtesy Library of Congress.)

The Greenbelt project employed both unskilled and skilled workers, such as this surveyor. Photographs like this would become iconic images of the New Deal as Roy Stryker, head of the Historical Section of the RA (later the Farm Security Administration), hired photographers to document the nation and many New Deal projects. Several of the photographers who documented Greenbelt went on to work for major American magazines, including John Vachon, Arthur Rothstein, and Marion Post Wolcott. (Courtesy Library of Congress, photograph by Carl Mydans.)

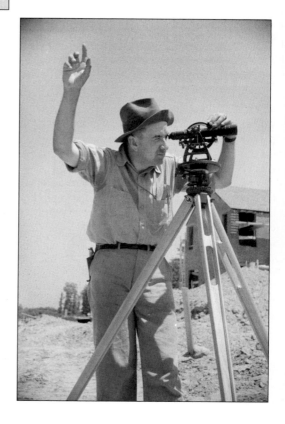

Two

BUILDING GREENBELT

Of the Resettlement Administration's three goals in building the greenbelt towns—to put people to work, to create housing for those of moderate incomes, and to demonstrate careful town planning—the first had the most immediate impact. Ground was broken in October 1935, construction began in February 1936, and from that point throughout construction of the town, the use of machinery was minimized. George Allen, head of the WPA District of Columbia Transient Bureau, reportedly brought workers to the site even before plans were finalized. Work for them was found, however, and they began, by hand, to clear the land that would become the lake. If a man could do the work of a machine, then a man did it. Located 13 miles northeast of Washington, DC, on 12,189 acres that had been purchased by the government (3,411 acres of which was reserved for Greenbelt), the project was massive in scope, and just getting workers to the site was a challenge. They were first bussed from Washington and Baltimore. Later, they travelled by train to the nearby Branchville station and were brought the rest of the way on trucks. The total cost of the original project was estimated to be between $13.45 million and $14 million, though relief labor was thought to account for roughly $5 million of that amount.

The Resettlement Administration also claimed that the project did more than just provide work for laborers; it also provided job training and allowed experimentation with new building materials. Cinder block, glass block, and copper piping, for instance, were incorporated into Greenbelt's construction. In the end, over 13,000 workers were employed at the Greenbelt site, making it one of the largest projects of the New Deal. The town was also constructed with sensitivity to the landscape. The main streets, Ridge and Crescent Roads, referenced the topography of the area. Ridge Road is higher and travels along a naturally occurring ridge that was not leveled during construction. Crescent Road is a curving horseshoe shape that flows around the town center. Several main cross streets then divide the town into roughly 14-acre superblocks that are significantly larger than standard city blocks and are one of Greenbelt's iconic features.

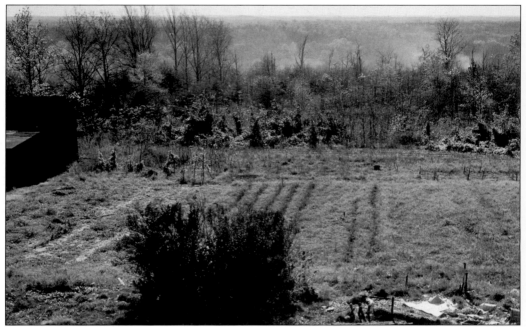

This image depicts some of the rolling hills, wooded areas, and worn-out tobacco farmland that would be transformed into Greenbelt as seen from Crabbe Place. The RA acquired a total of 12,189 acres for the project, which was intended to include areas for housing, parks, allotment gardens, small farms, and areas for expansion. (Courtesy Library of Congress, photograph by Carl Mydans.)

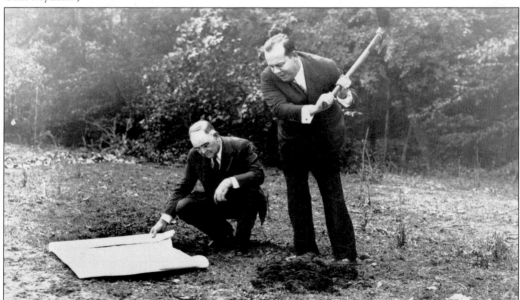

On October 12, 1935, officials first broke ground for the Greenbelt project; Dr. Will Alexander is on the left, and George E. Allen, the DC administrator of the Works Progress Administration, is on the right. According to the *Washington Star* newspaper, Allen was reported to have said that the Greenbelt project solved "the greatest single relief problem which the District Government faces." (Courtesy Library of Congress, photograph by Elmer Johnson.)

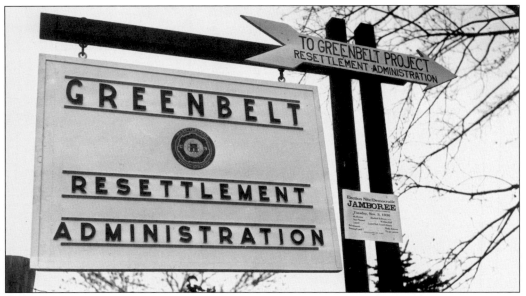

Despite the fact that ground for the project was broken in 1935, it was not until January 1936 that the project was officially given the name Greenbelt. Prior to that, it was sometimes referred to as the Berwyn Project, because Berwyn Heights was the nearest town to the construction site. (Courtesy Library of Congress.)

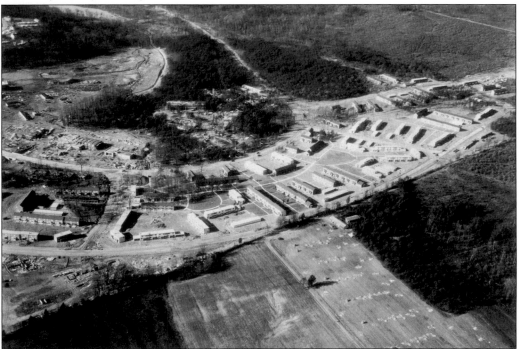

This aerial view shows how Greenbelt was carved out of a rural landscape. When this photograph was taken, the housing courts had begun to take shape, as had the central buildings. About 12,000 to 13,000 plants, shrubs, and small trees were moved to a nursery and then replaced as construction was finished. Angus MacGregor, who reportedly had held positions with J. Pierpont Morgan, among others, was the head gardener. (Courtesy Library of Congress.)

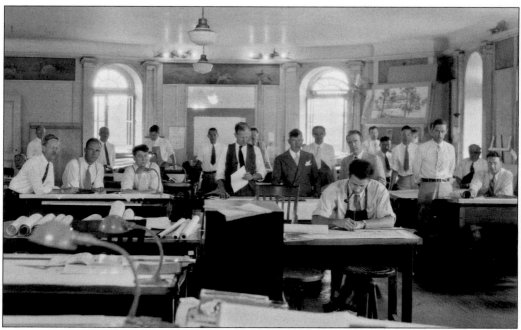

Architects, draftsmen, and others worked on plans for Greenbelt from the Evelyn Walsh McLean mansion in Washington, DC, as seen above. Because Greenbelt was a relief project and many laborers were brought to the site each day from Washington, DC, and Baltimore eager to work, plans had to be rushed to the site as soon as they were done. According to O. Kline Fulmer, an architect on the project and later an assistant community manager, there was "a spectacular race between the architects and the construction engineers. . . . Plans were rushed to the blueprinters almost before the last lines were drawn." (Both, courtesy Library of Congress.)

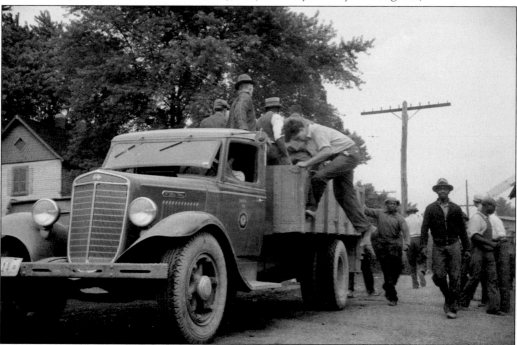

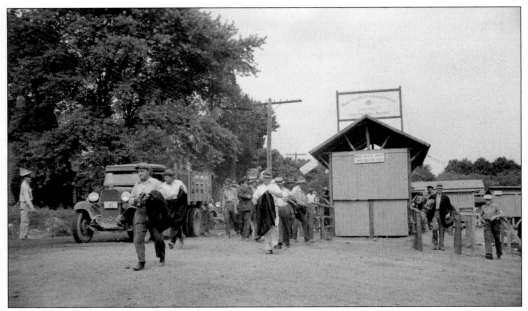

Workers were divided into three groups and given different colored badges to wear: white for unskilled, yellow for semiskilled, and red for skilled. A sign urged workers to "wear badges where they can be seen." Unskilled workers employed to build Greenbelt made between 51¢ and 57¢ an hour. A skilled workman could make up to $1.50 an hour. Also, in order to give everyone a chance to work, the laborers were divided into shifts. (Courtesy Library of Congress.)

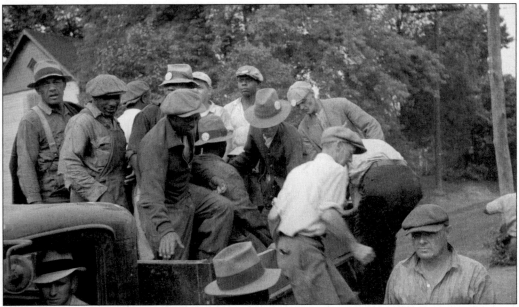

Workers lived in lodges in Washington, DC, and though they appear to have been transported together, the several hundred African Americans were reportedly housed separately. At the start, it was reported that morale in the African American lodge was low, but as the project got underway, morale improved. According to historian Joseph Arnold, the men had "formed their own policing system and lodge council . . . and organized sports teams, purchased equipment for the lodge and even put on a vaudeville show." (Courtesy Library of Congress.)

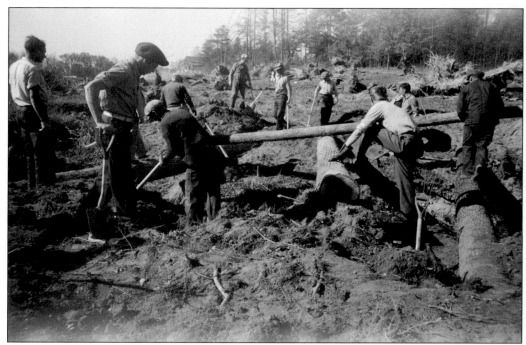

One of the first projects at the Greenbelt site was the creation of a lake. Originally a heavily wooded 23-acre valley cut by a stream, the lake required a year and over 200 men to complete it. Because the federal government was interested in putting as many unemployed laborers to work as possible, much of the land was cleared by hand. Men pulled the trees and stumps out by their roots and cleared the brush. Some of the wood was given to relief agencies to be used as firewood, while some was burned at the site. (Both, courtesy Library of Congress.)

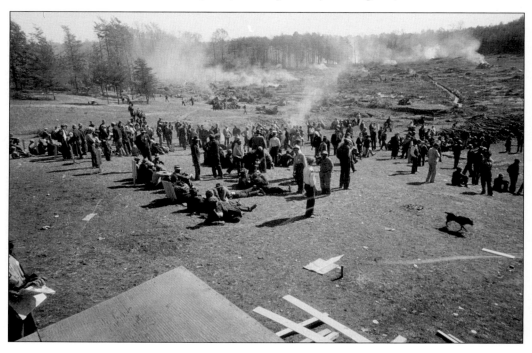

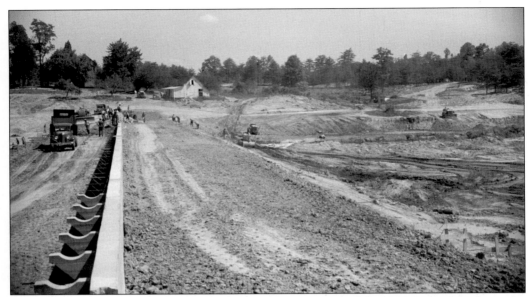

Workers built a 22-foot dam on the east side of what is now the lake. Today, the dam forms the eastern link of a one-and-a-quarter-mile walking path that encircles the lake. (Courtesy Library of Congress.)

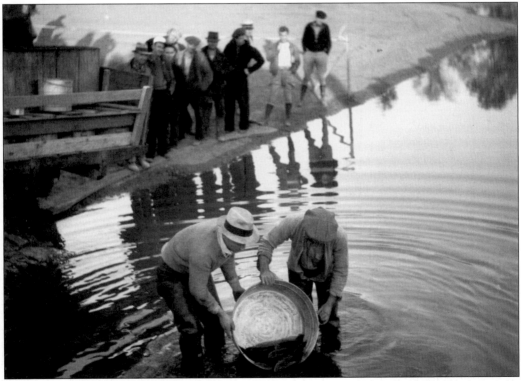

Once completed, the lake was stocked with fish. Pres. Franklin D. Roosevelt presided over the introduction of the first fish into the lake when he visited in November 1936. Fishing has long been a favorite lake activity. The Bureau of Fisheries stocked the new lake with bluegills, perch, catfish, crappie, sunfish, and bass. (Courtesy Library of Congress.)

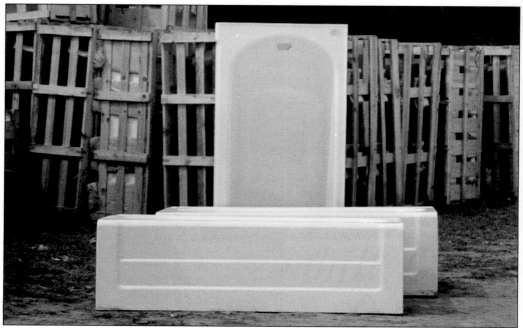

Building materials, including bathtubs and steel casement windows, were delivered and stacked on-site. Each housing unit in Greenbelt was equipped with indoor plumbing and a streamlined, built-in bathtub, though no showerheads were included in the design. Inclusion of a built-in tub was the latest in bathroom design in the mid-1930s, and many homes retain their original bathtubs today. Sturdy steel casement windows would let in a maximum of amount light and air, which was important to Greenbelt's planners. (Both, courtesy Library of Congress, photographs by Carl Mydans.)

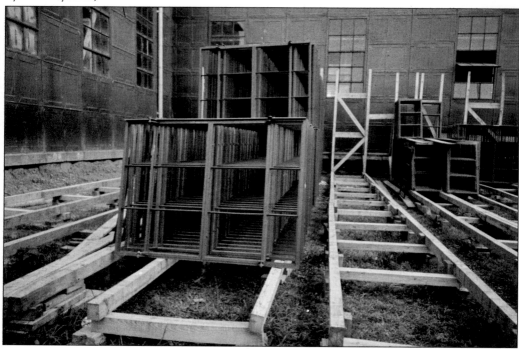

Rexford Guy Tugwell oversees construction on a visit to the Greenbelt site. Tugwell, a former economics professor at Columbia, was known for his white suits, controversial ideas, and what some considered a brusque manner. Criticism of his policies and initiatives eventually became too great, and he resigned from the RA at the end of 1936. (Courtesy Library of Congress, photograph by ? Brooks.)

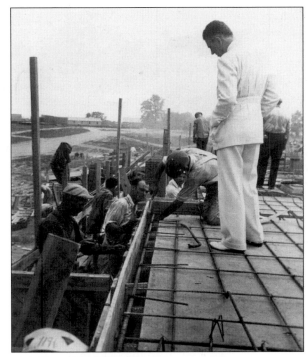

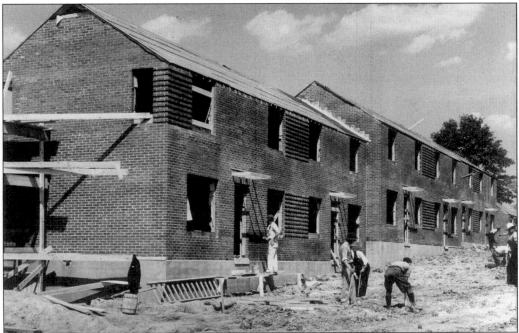

During the construction of Greenbelt, 574 row houses, 306 garden apartments, and 5 prefabricated single-family houses were built. According to a Farm Security Administration report, "The use of different materials and varying colors of paint helps to give the houses in all the towns an individual appearance. . . . All of the houses were placed to get the most sunlight and windows were arranged to catch the prevailing breeze and look out on attractive landscapes." (Courtesy Tugwell Room, Greenbelt branch of Prince George's County Memorial Library.)

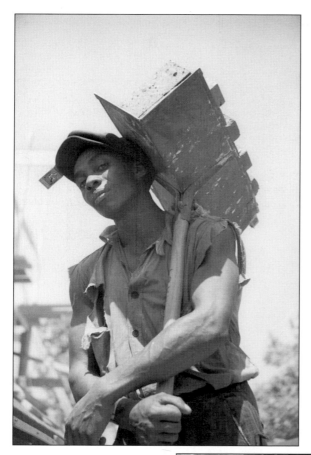

These men were some of the minority construction workers who helped build Greenbelt. Though African American workers helped construct the town, they were not allowed to apply for residency, as both the county and state were racially segregated at the time. However, there were two other late-1930s New Deal housing projects for African Americans in the mid-Atlantic region. Langston Terrace was an apartment complex in Washington, DC, and Newport News Homesteads (now called Aberdeen Gardens) was a project built by and for African Americans outside of that city in Virginia. (Left, courtesy Library of Congress; below, courtesy Greenbelt Museum.)

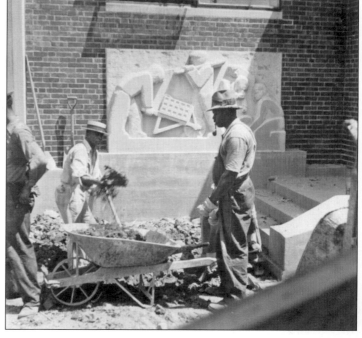

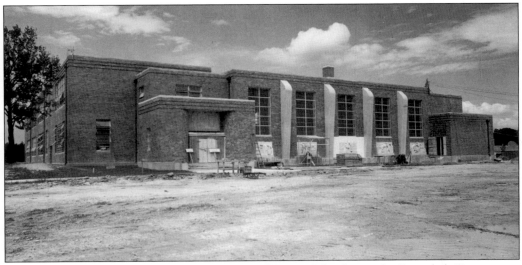

Lenore Thomas sculpted bas-reliefs on the front of Center School, now the Greenbelt Community Center. Given complete freedom to choose her subject matter, she chose the preamble to the US Constitution. She believed that American schoolchildren needed to learn about the foundations of their country and political system. Thomas worked on several government projects during the Depression. It took her and an assistant over a year to complete the reliefs. While working on them, Thomas remarked, "We want to keep the designs bold and simple and sufficiently obvious so that, with the lettering beneath each panel, any workman or child can understand them. After we finish blocking out the figures we are going to use the workmen around here [as models] for the faces and costumes." (Both, courtesy Greenbelt Museum.)

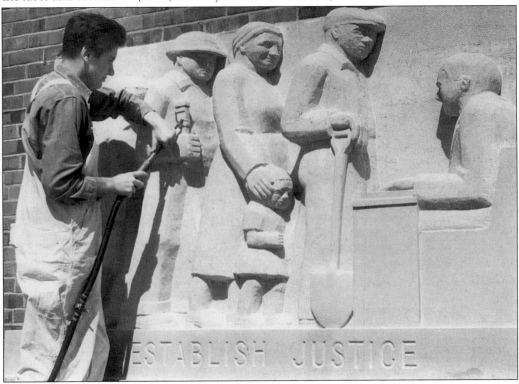

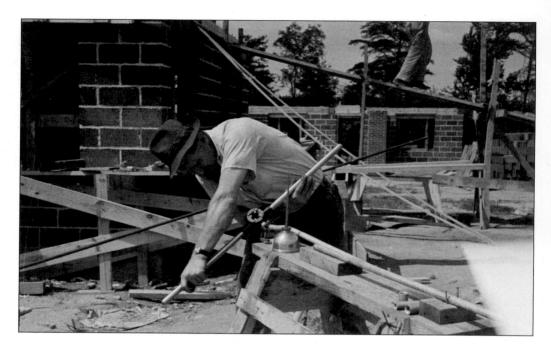

The final stages of construction were done by the most skilled workers: electricians, plumbers, and plasterers. To preserve the plaster walls once tenants moved in, each room in the housing units had picture molding near the ceiling, allowing families to easily hang or change artwork in the rooms without putting nail holes in the walls. The government also used high-quality materials where possible with the understanding that those of modest incomes would not be able to afford to make repairs to their homes. (Both, courtesy Library of Congress.)

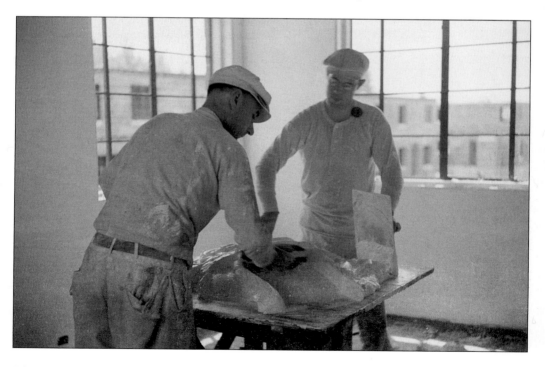

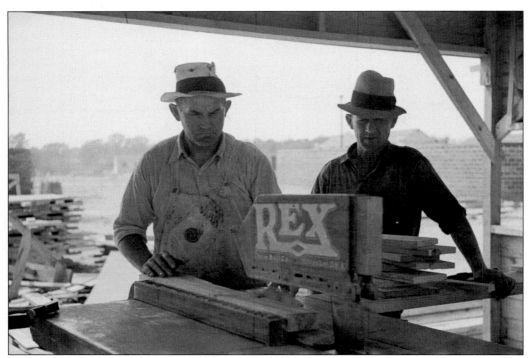

Workers cut wood for the housing project. Note the RA badge worn by the worker on the left. (Courtesy Library of Congress, photograph by Carl Mydans.)

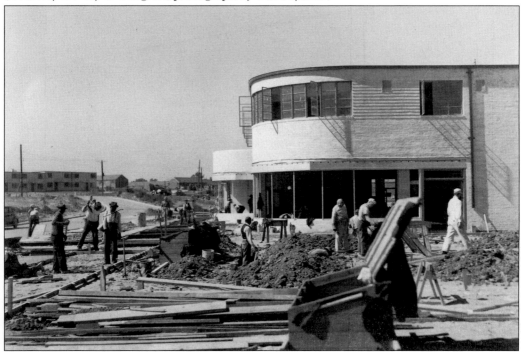

This scene shows construction taking place in the center of town, which would house stores and other services for the townspeople. The large curving facade was mirrored on the opposite side, creating a dramatic entryway to the commercial center. (Courtesy Greenbelt Museum.)

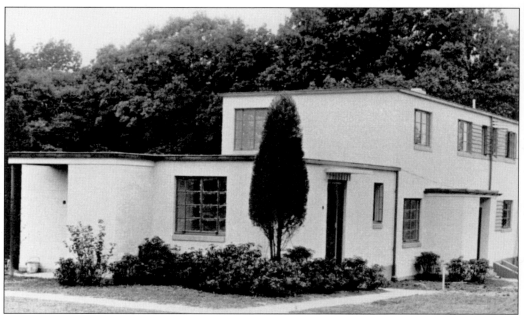

The architecture in Greenbelt has been described many ways. In an article in the town newspaper, the *Cooperator*, O. Kline Fulmer described it simply as "functional, if you must put a name to it." He went on to write, "Contemporary is also another name which could be used truthfully as a description of the style, but any other name, such as English, Modernistic, Continental, etc., implies a false stylizing of surface treatment that is entirely erroneous." (Courtesy Library of Congress.)

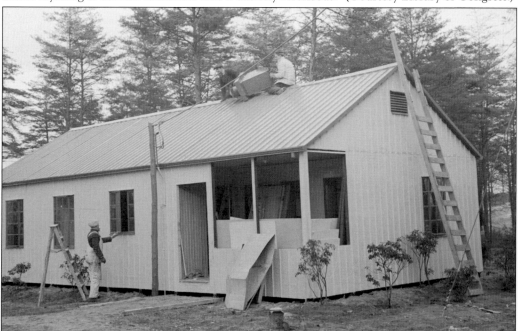

Many relatively new building materials were first experimented with at Greenbelt, including cinder block, copper pipe, and glass block. In addition to the other forms of housing, the federal government built five prefabricated single-family units made of steel. (Courtesy Library of Congress, photograph by Arthur Rothstein.)

In 1938, General Houses of Chicago, Inc., owned by the Fisher Brothers, built 10 experimental streamlined homes that were composed of concrete slabs, steel frames, and prefabricated panels. General Houses had exhibited a nearly identical model to the ones built in Greenbelt in the Homes of Tomorrow Exhibition at the 1933 Chicago Century of Progress Exposition. The photograph at right shows how the panels were added to the steel frames. (Both, courtesy Greenbelt Museum.)

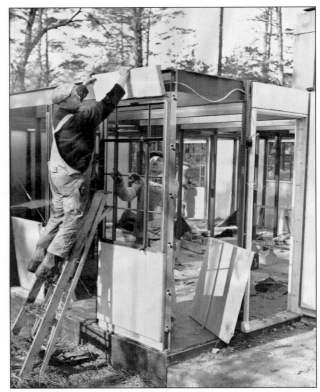

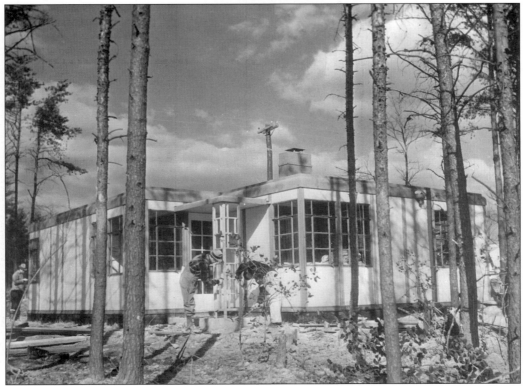

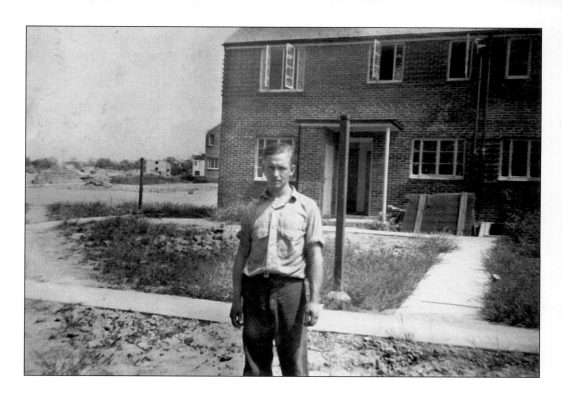

These snapshots were taken by one of the workers on the Greenbelt project, Richard Hughes. The shopping center was still under construction as of February 1937; note the tape over the large curved windows and the absence of the theater marquee. By the time families arrived in the fall, however, the center was ready. One contemporary observer wrote in an article in the *Digest*, "At the center of the town the gleaming white business and community buildings curve graciously around a plaza." (Both, courtesy Greenbelt Museum.)

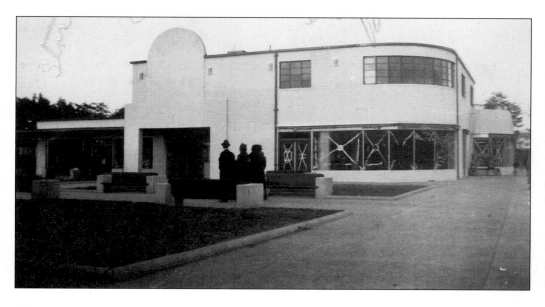

Painting the houses was one of the last phases of construction. House exteriors were painted white, but bright colors were used to highlight the brick detailing around and between the windows. Several oral history accounts mention the bright trim, which must have been striking against the stark white buildings. According to early resident Janet James, "the little lines that look like rows of bricks sticking out between the windows were painted pastels, each building having the same color for all. Some were pink, some delicate yellow, some light green and some light blue. It seemed to me that I remember some orchid too. I thought it was right pretty, but my father said it was too effeminate and not the colors a man would want on his house." (Both, courtesy Library of Congress; below, photograph by Arthur Rothstein.)

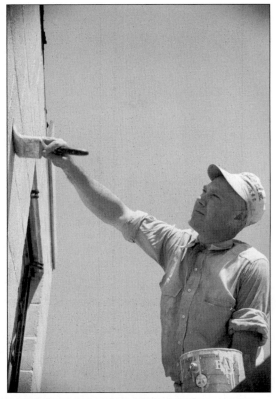

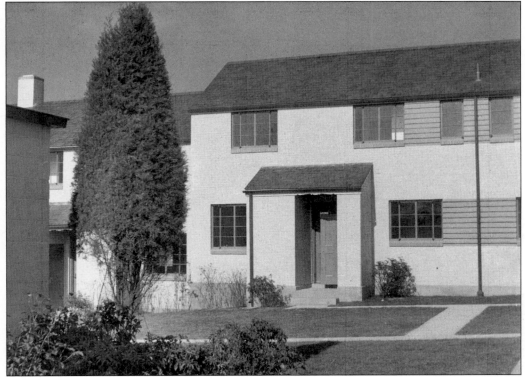

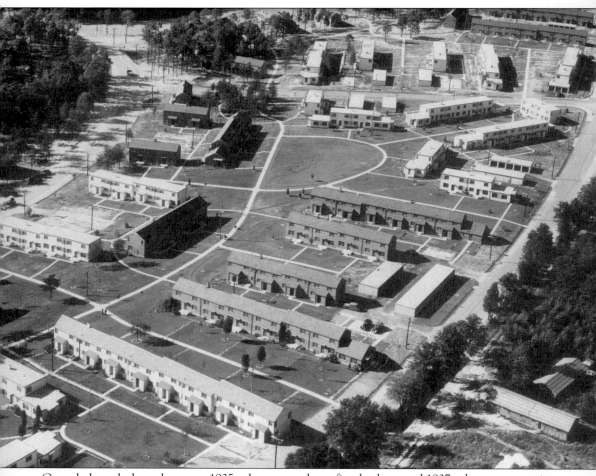

Greenbelt took shape between 1935, when ground was first broken, and 1937, when construction was largely completed. This aerial shot shows the carefully placed rows of houses, gently curving streets, and walkways that wound through superblocks and expanses of green space. (Courtesy Library of Congress.)

Three

GREENBELT PIONEERS SETTLE IN

By late 1937, the federal government's careful planning and construction of Greenbelt was coming to fruition. Houses, roads, schools, and a shopping area had all been completed. The Resettlement Administration received over 5,000 applications for the 885 units constructed, and the selection committee screened applicants carefully, leading critics to accuse the government of social engineering. Each family filled out an application and was interviewed, and in some cases, a member of the trained staff of the 30-person selection committee visited the family's current home. Heads of household had to be gainfully employed, earning between $800 and $2,200 per year. Greenbelt's first families, or pioneers, as they would be called, began moving on September 30, 1937. By June 1938, 610 families consisting of 2,300 people had moved in; when all 885 families had moved in, the town's population became 3,000. Although they were all white families, as Greenbelt was segregated at the time, they represented a cross section of the Washington, DC, region in terms of religion, which was remarkable for the time period. Protestants, Catholics, and Jews found themselves living side by side.

The federal government, intent that Greenbelt should succeed, put in place strict guidelines and regulations concerning everything from when and where laundry could be hung to what size family was appropriate for each unit. Cooperative businesses were encouraged and even nurtured until residents could take them over, and the Center School, as it was called, busy with students by day, also became a thriving community center each evening where the many organizations Greenbelters formed could meet. Residents made the most of the copious green space included in the town plan, and children played freely throughout the community. Though huge changes would come by the beginning of the 1940s with the advent of war, many of Greenbelt's most important and long-lasting organizations were rooted, well established, and poised to flourish despite the challenges ahead.

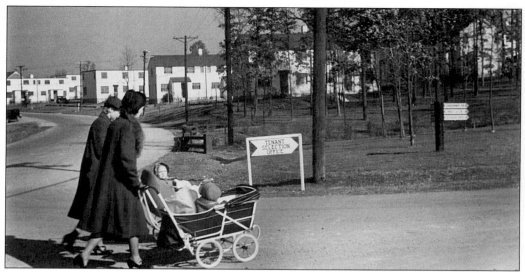

The first residents of Greenbelt were rigorously screened. Applicants filled out surveys, were interviewed by the Farm Security Administration's family selection specialists, and occasionally had their homes inspected; the head of the household also had to be employed. In addition, the selection committee was looking for residents who would be willing to participate in cooperative businesses and community activities. When additional housing was added in 1941, this intensive screening process was not continued. (Courtesy Library of Congress, photograph by John Vachon.)

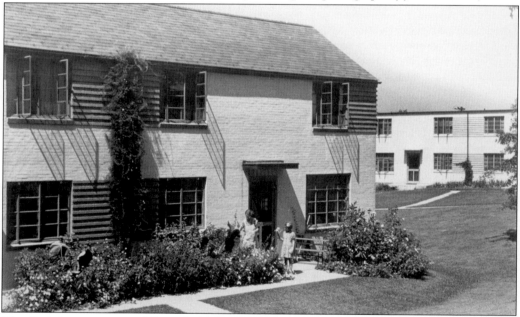

The Steinles were one of Greenbelt's early families who moved from a small apartment in Washington, DC. Louise Steinle Winker, pictured here with her mother, recalled the move, "I remember taking what seemed like forever to drive to Greenbelt to look at the model home. It was the home we moved into a short time later. . . . It was nothing to compare with the cramped quarters we had. . . . Best of all we would no longer have to share a bathroom with three or four other families." David Steinle, an avid gardener, won awards for the family's beautiful yard. (Courtesy Library of Congress, photograph by Marion Post Wolcott.)

Oral histories reveal that Greenbelt's housewives were delighted with their small but efficient kitchens, which included electric stoves and refrigerators. The local electric company held periodic classes in the early years instructing women on how to use their electric appliances. Women also formed what were called Better Buyers groups, where they judged and tested canned foods and researched milk grading. Neighbors also helped one another in more casual ways. In this photograph from 1938, Mrs. Stanley Rider offers tips to Marna Jacobsen, who was reportedly the town's first bride. (Courtesy Greenbelt Museum.)

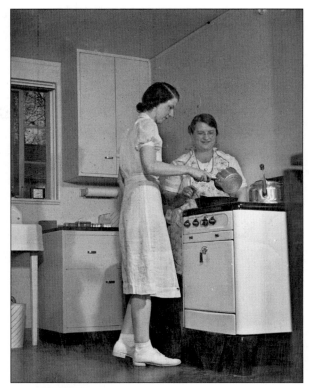

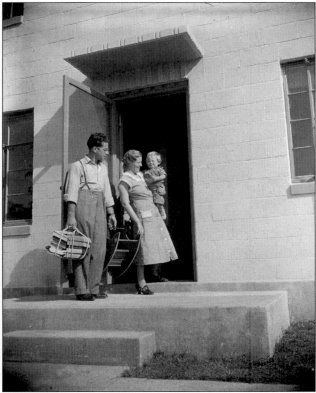

The first families to move to Greenbelt are often referred to as pioneers. Early Greenbelters thought of themselves as pioneers "of a new way of living," as a poem written by Mary E. Van Cleve that was published in a 1937 edition of the town newspaper, the *Cooperator*, described it. Here, Irving Machiz with his wife and son, Edward, carry belongings into their unit in October 1937. (Courtesy Library of Congress.)

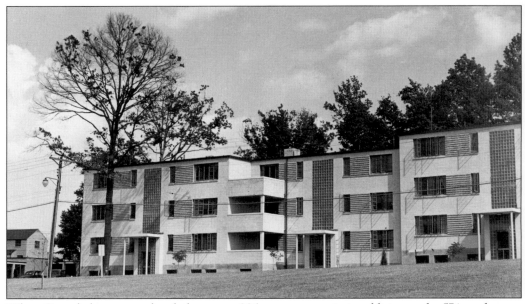

When Greenbelt was completed, there were 306 apartment units in addition to the 574 row homes. Rents for both ranged from $31.50 to $41 per month. The apartment buildings featured studio apartments, one-bedroom, and two-bedroom units. The majority of apartments were occupied by single people or young couples without children. Huge expanses of glass block at the apartment entrances allowed natural light to illuminate the stairways, and many apartments featured terraces. (Courtesy Greenbelt Museum.)

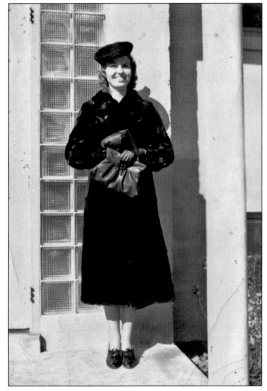

John and Edith Frank moved to Greenbelt in the spring of 1938. They were the first family to occupy an apartment at 4A Parkway. Edith Frank recalled, "Our apartment in Takoma Park was costing us half of my husband's salary. When someone told us about Greenbelt, we immediately applied. . . . The houses were already occupied and we were the first family to move into an apartment. . . . There was a very large attractive playground right outside and I could watch through the window as Ray played." John Frank, who captured this image, would go on to be a photographer for the Air Force in World War II. (Courtesy John Ray Frank.)

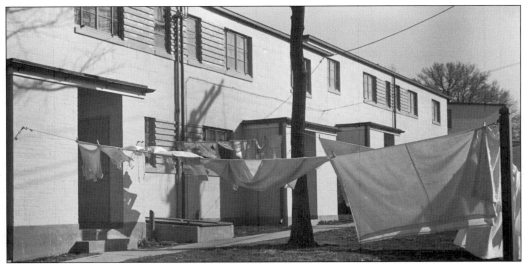

Greenbelt would become well known for its early rules, many of which involved laundry. Laundry lines on the service side of the house were to be kept taut, as no sagging was allowed. Additionally, clothing had to be removed by 4:00 p.m. each day, and no laundry could be hung on Sundays. While restrictive, these rules were taken seriously by most residents, as they kept the town looking orderly, a contrast to scenes of overcrowded, chaotic inner-city life with laundry lines hanging haphazardly between buildings. (Courtesy Library of Congress, photograph by John Vachon.)

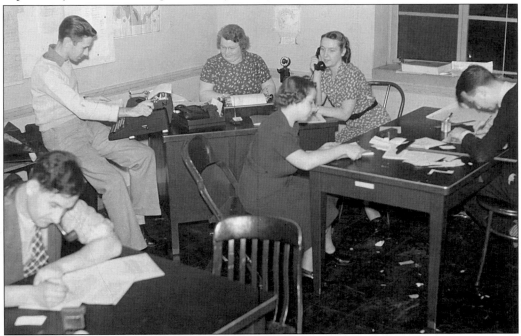

In their first years in the town, Greenbelt residents formed over 50 organizations and clubs. The Journalistic Club, formed on November 11, 1937, was not only one of the first but arguably one of the most important, as it would produce the town newspaper, the *Cooperator*. Originally started in a Greenbelt living room, the paper today is called the *Greenbelt News Review*, is staffed by dedicated volunteers, is run as a cooperative, and has never missed an issue since November 1937. (Courtesy Library of Congress, photograph by Marjory Collins.)

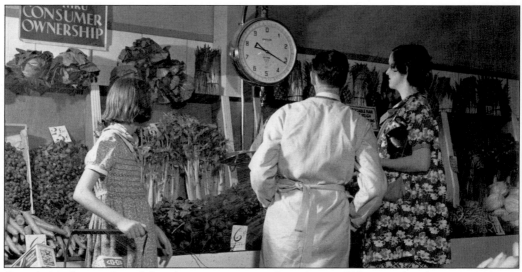

Greenbelt's planners hoped that the various stores and services would be owned and run cooperatively by the residents who utilized them. Boston merchant and philanthropist Edward Filene loaned the residents funds to establish the businesses. In 1940, Greenbelt citizens organized the Greenbelt Consumer Cooperative and purchased Greenbelt Consumer Services (GCS). GCS businesses included a grocery store, a gas station, a drugstore, a barbershop, a movie theater, a valet shop, a beauty parlor, a variety store, and a tobacco shop, all in or near the center of town. The Greenbelt Co-op Supermarket featured shopping carts, billed at the time as a modern convenience, and shoppers could choose items for themselves. According to a writer for the *Cooperator*, "Shopping in Greenbelt is going to be such fun. . . . And everyone seems to be pleased with the self-service idea and the traveling market-baskets." Though the original co-op store burned in 1962 and the organizing cooperative has changed over the years, the Greenbelt Co-op was rebuilt, it is still a cooperative business, and it remains popular today. (Above, courtesy Greenbelt Museum; below, courtesy Library of Congress, photograph by Russel Lee.)

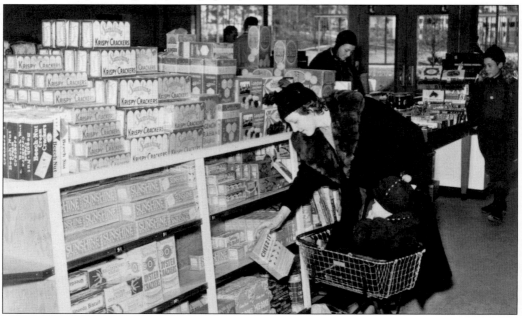

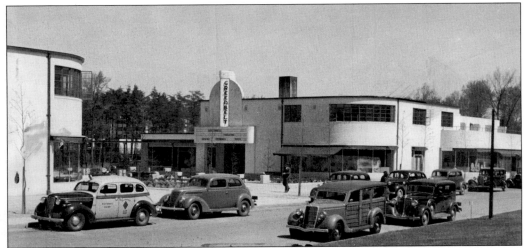

Like the other businesses in the center, the theater was a cooperative. Members voted on which films would be shown, the cost of admission, and concessions. The theater opened in September 1938, and the first movie shown was Shirley Temple's *Little Miss Broadway*. In 2000, the marquee was restored, and in 2002, the building was purchased by the City of Greenbelt, ensuring that its operation would continue. (Courtesy Greenbelt Museum.)

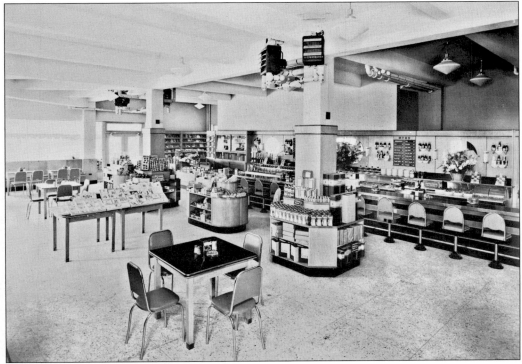

Greenbelt's drugstore and soda fountain, pristine in 1937, would become a popular meeting place for Greenbelt residents of all ages. It also offered employment. Louise Steinle Winker, a pioneer resident, recalled, "My mother got a job in the drug store as the manager of the soda fountain and a little later we kids had the thrill of ordering a sandwich and soda and sitting at the counter. It was our first experience in eating out." The drugstore and soda fountain went out of business in the 1960s. (Courtesy Greenbelt Museum.)

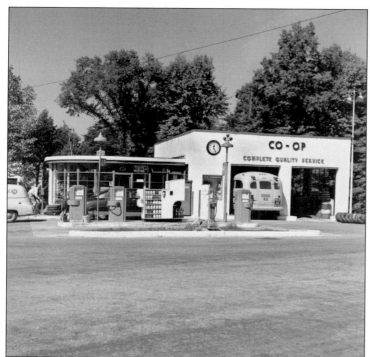

Greenbelt Consumer Services also opened a gas station in 1937. In 1939, when owning a car was still considered a luxury, 65 percent of Greenbelt households owned one. In 1938, the gas station charged $1.25 for an oil change, and gasoline was 23¢ per gallon. In the cooperative spirit, many Greenbelters carpooled to work. Residents could also take a bus to nearby Branchville that connected with the streetcar line to get to jobs in Washington, DC. (Courtesy Greenbelt Museum, photograph by Paul Kasko.)

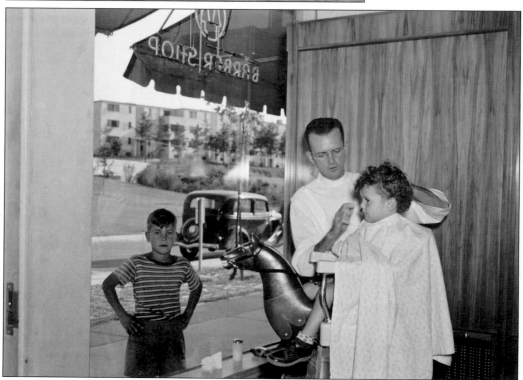

Louis Mead, age 2 years, 3 months old, gets a haircut in this photograph from 1939. The twin pine tree neon sign in the window was the logo for Greenbelt Consumer Services, the overarching cooperative that ran the stores in the center for many years. (Courtesy Greenbelt Museum.)

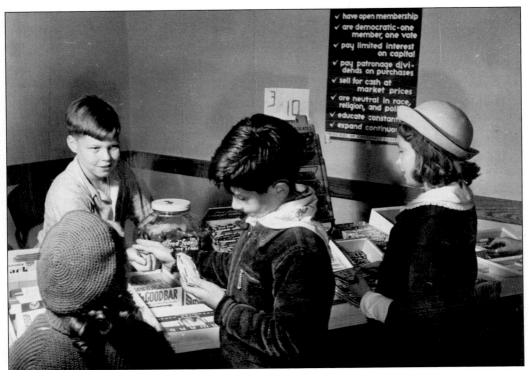

Greenbelt's children were caught up in the cooperative spirit as well. Center School had a progressive philosophy, and under Principal Catherine T. Reed, the children learned by doing projects and exploring nature. In 1937, elementary students established what they called the "gum drop co-op" and sold candy, paper, and pencils. Just as with the other cooperatives, a percentage of the profits went back to its members. (Courtesy Greenbelt Museum.)

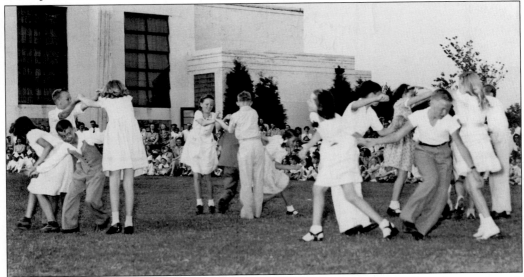

Center School was used for adult education, religious services, and meetings in the evenings. It also housed Prince George's County's first kindergarten, established in 1938. During the spring, students celebrated May Day, May 1, with dances on the lawn in front of the school. (Courtesy Greenbelt Museum.)

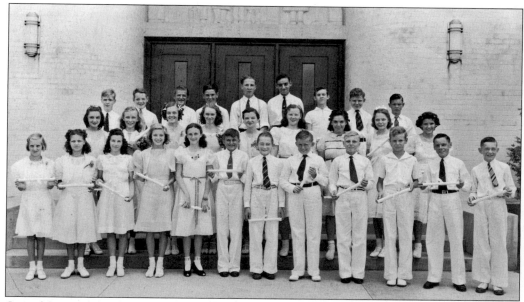

One of Center School's first graduating classes proudly hold their diplomas in front of the building. Students went on to Greenbelt High School, which was open until 1954, when the school became a middle school and upper class students went to nearby High Point High School. As the number of students grew, the building also grew, with a new wing added onto the building's north side. Today, the building is a thriving community center that, following restoration, opened in 1995. (Courtesy Greenbelt Museum.)

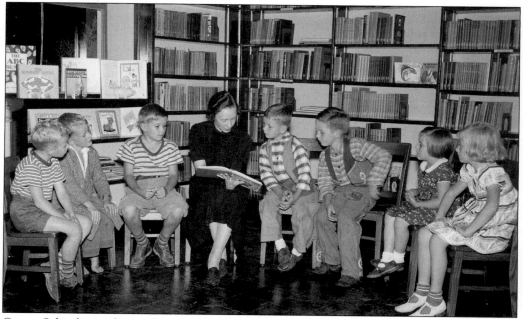

Center School served many functions for Greenbelt's early residents. The town library was housed there beginning in 1939. A county branch of the library system opened in Greenbelt in 1970. In this photograph from 1939, students gather for a story hour. Planners had also intended from the start that the building would be used by adults in the evening for meetings. In early maps, the building is listed as "Center School and Community Building." (Courtesy Greenbelt Museum.)

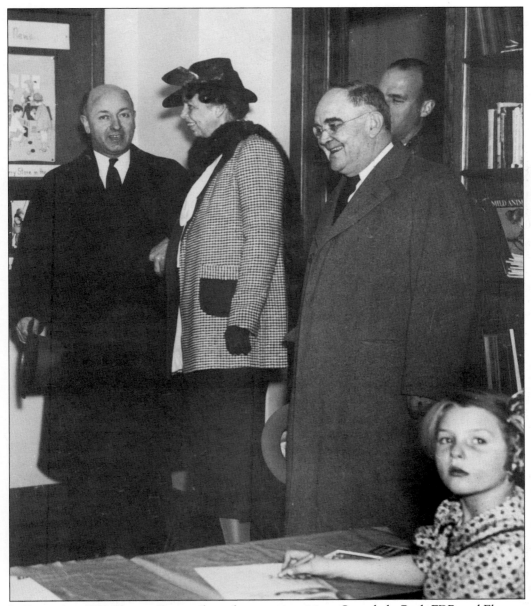

In December 1937, Eleanor Roosevelt made a surprise visit to Greenbelt. Both FDR and Eleanor had taken an interest in Greenbelt's progress from its beginning. The first lady toured Center School with FSA official Will Alexander, right, and town manager Roy Braden, left. Her interest in the town was far from just theoretical. In 1937, the RA was reorganized into the FSA and completion of the project was jeopardized. Wallace Richards, the RA executive formerly in charge of Greenbelt, wrote to Eleanor Roosevelt for help, as many amenities such as the swimming pool, playgrounds, landscaping, and allotment gardens were threatened. Richards wrote, "last minute economy would affect those very things which we had counted on to hold the townsfolk at home, make them happy and community conscious, and prevent them from spending a disproportionate amount of their income in seeking relaxation elsewhere." In response, the first lady wrote to FDR and ensured that Greenbelt's recreational spaces were completed as planned. (Courtesy Greenbelt Museum.)

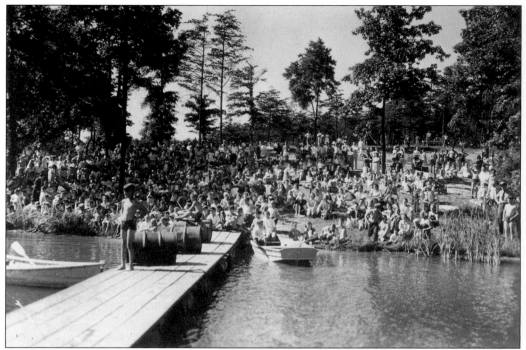

Due to Eleanor Roosevelt's intervention, Greenbelt's recreational spaces were saved, and the community has continued to gather, for instance, at the lake for the Fourth of July, as pictured above in 1938, or for picnics, parties, and barbecues under the pavilion (below) that once stood on the grounds but has since been torn down. (Both, courtesy Greenbelt Museum; above, photograph by Paul Kasko.)

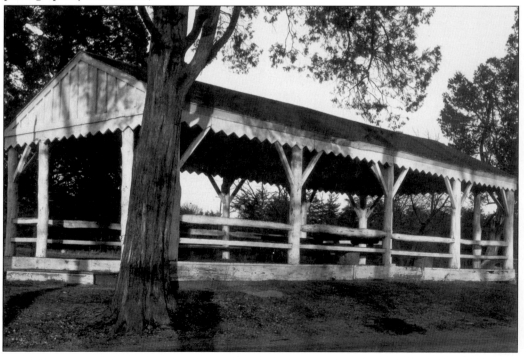

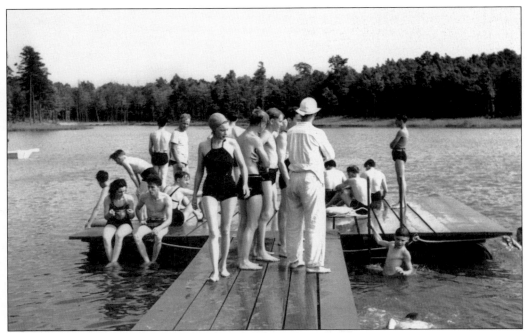

Swimming was popular at the lake when Greenbelt first opened. Lifeguards were employed to ensure swimmers' safety. Swimming was banned, however, in July 1938, as health officials soon discovered that the lake contained bacteria that made the water unsafe for swimming. (Courtesy Greenbelt Museum, photograph by Paul Kasko.)

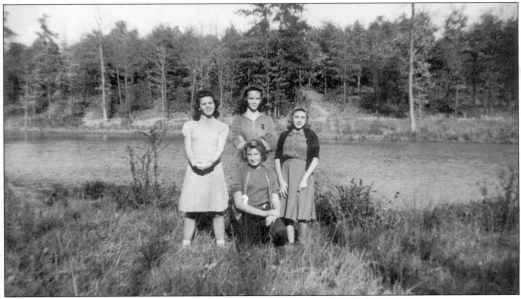

Marion Benson Hastings, who grew up in Greenbelt, took this photograph of friends at the Greenbelt Lake. Though swimming at the lake was banned, it was still a beloved recreation spot. Marion kept a diary as a young girl and mentioned the lake frequently. In one entry she wrote, "Walked over to the center tonight, then went with the gang over to the lake pavilion to dance. We danced to Dave's portable [radio]." (Courtesy Greenbelt Museum, photograph by Marion Benson Hastings.)

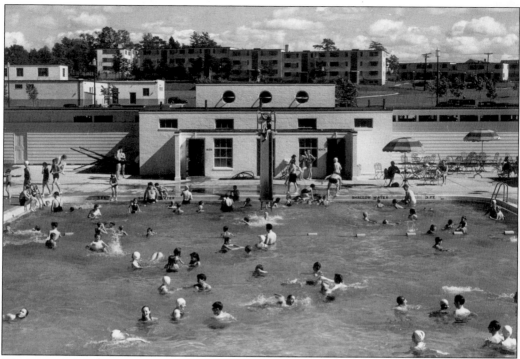

The Greenbelt pool contributed to what one early resident called the country club–like atmosphere of early Greenbelt. It was unusual for a housing project constructed for those of moderate incomes to have such amenities. Greenbelt's original outdoor swimming pool, opened on Memorial Day 1939, was only one of two public pools in the area. The other was at Glen Echo, Maryland. It was 120 feet long and 60 feet wide, and its deepest point was 9 feet. Marion Benson (second from left) was photographed at the pool with Don Whitamore (left), Doris Asher, and Pete Labukas. Residents also enjoyed a handball court, tennis courts, horseshoe pits, playgrounds, and baseball diamonds. (Both, courtesy Greenbelt Museum.)

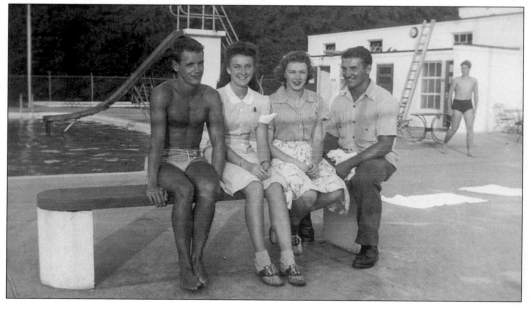

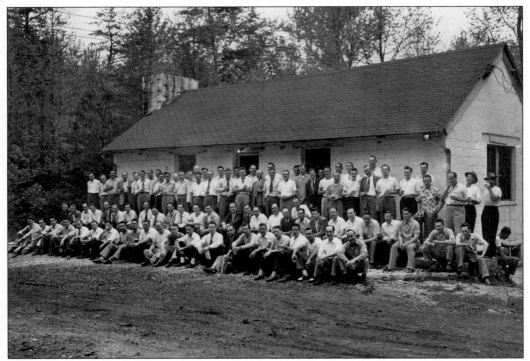

In addition to the cooperatives, citizens associations, hobby groups, and other organizations that formed, Greenbelters organized team sports as well. The Greenbelt Athletic Club, pictured above, was formed in February 1938 and had representatives from each block. For men, there was a basketball league, a volleyball league, and a softball league. The women's version offered volleyball, badminton, bowling, dance, and exercise classes. (Both, courtesy Greenbelt Museum.)

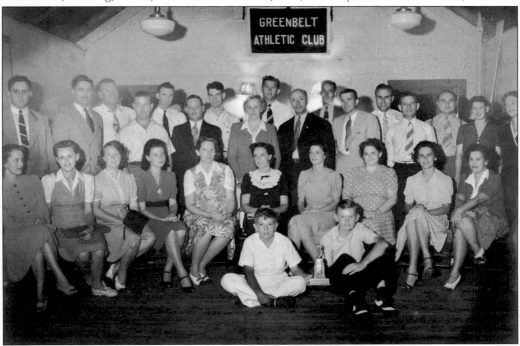

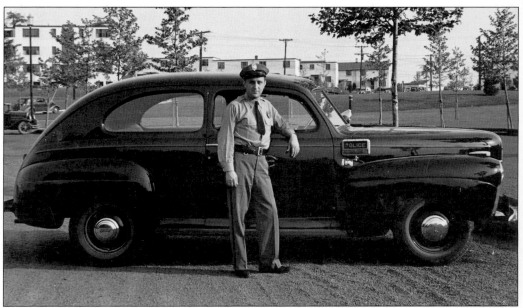

The Farm Security Administration had designed a town charter and submitted it to the State of Maryland prior to families moving in. On June, 1, 1937, Greenbelt became the first municipality in Maryland to be chartered with a council-manager form of government. George Panagoulis, pictured here with a police cruiser, was appointed the first police officer in December 1937. During the next year, two more policemen were added: Yale Huffman and Albert "Buddy" Attick. (Courtesy Greenbelt Museum.)

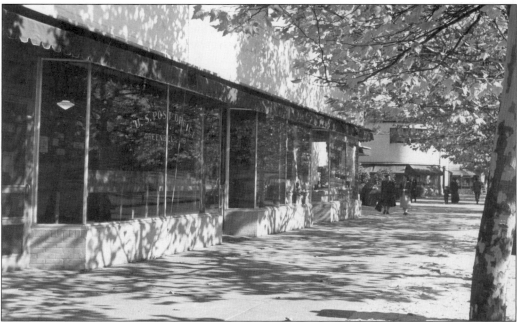

The Greenbelt Post Office opened in September 1937 as the first residents arrived. It was a fourth-class office, however, so mail was not delivered to homes, and all residents had to visit the post office to pick up their mail, something which many Greenbelt pioneer children fondly remember. (Courtesy Greenbelt Museum.)

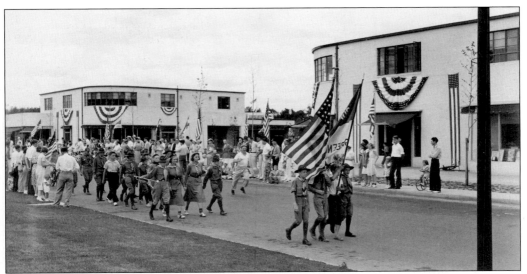

Though one of Greenbelt's beloved traditions, the weekend-long Labor Day festival would not officially begin until 1955; Greenbelt's first town fair was a forerunner that took place September 7–9, 1939. The Greenbelt Garden Club requested in spring that the council support a flower and garden contest to be scheduled for fall, and that request led to the fair, which featured flower, garden, baking, needlework, and athletic contests. In addition, there were parades, dancing, concerts, and exhibits, such as the one pictured below, which addressed religious life. Although Greenbelt was segregated racially, it was from the very beginning integrated in terms of religion. Greenbelt's planners had attempted to populate the town with a cross section of religions that reflected the general Washington, DC, area: 63 percent Protestant, 37 percent Catholic, and 7 percent Jewish. No religious buildings were built initially because of the separation of church and state, but services for Protestants and Jews were held in the school/community center, while Catholics worshiped in the theater. Greenbelt's early religious leaders formed the Permanent Conference on Religious Life to broaden understanding of religion. They produced the exhibit pictured below in 1939. (Both, courtesy Greenbelt Museum.)

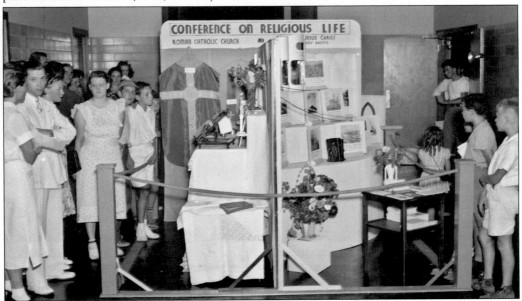

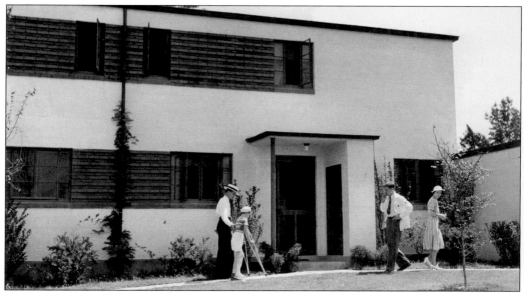

On April 1, 1938, the Greenbelt Health Association, a venture in cooperative health care, opened in two converted row houses. One hundred fifty of the 490 families then living in Greenbelt joined, and by 1940, it had expanded to 377 families. The membership fee was $5, then $2 monthly for families and $1.50 for individuals. The hospital facility included two operating rooms, an x-ray room, a kitchen, and a laboratory. Financial difficulties forced the facility to close in 1942, and the health association was dissolved in 1950. (Courtesy Library of Congress.)

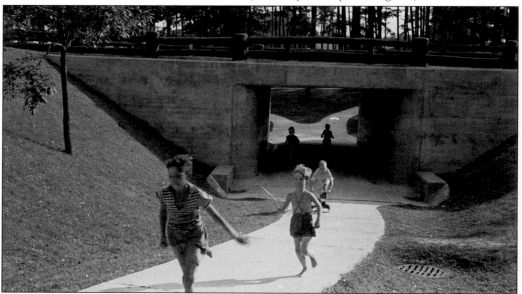

Children who grew up in Greenbelt speak of the unusual freedom they had to roam safely throughout the town. The underpasses that were included in Greenbelt's plan were instrumental in this freedom. Children featured prominently in the 1939 documentary film *The City*. Filmed partially in Greenbelt, it portrayed the community as the town of tomorrow and was shown at the 1939 New York World's Fair. Greenbelt pioneer child Bob Sommers was in the film, along with several other Greenbelt youngsters. They were paid 25¢ per day. (Courtesy Library of Congress, photograph by Marion Post Wolcott.)

Four

WORLD WAR II AND THE 1940S

World War II had an immense impact on Greenbelt, Maryland, just as it did on so many communities across the nation. In Greenbelt, however, changes came very early, as the federal government announced in February 1941 that 1,000 additional homes would be built in Greenbelt to house wartime workers. One of 43 defense housing projects in the United States, the homes would be funded by the $150-million Lanham Act. The additional homes nearly doubled Greenbelt's population. The government's intent was to maintain the model design of the original part of the town, and the homes were arranged in courts within superblocks that featured shared green space. However, neither the walkways that wound through the original part of town nor the underpasses were utilized, and budget limitations resulted in only modest landscaping. The intense screening process was also relaxed, though residency was only open to military personnel and civilians working for the Army and Navy departments, and annual income had to be below $2,600 per year. Nevertheless, the residents of the frame homes, as they were called because of the style of their construction, became absorbed by the town, and residents together participated in the blackout drills, rationing, Victory Gardens, and scrap-metal drives that occupied Greenbelt during the war.

The increased population did pose several challenges for the town. Greenbelt Consumer Services opened a store in converted row houses in the North End, as the area was called, and an additional elementary school was also built there. The schools were forced to run multiple shifts of students. Greenbelt had a relatively young population, so an unusually high number of residents joined the Armed Forces. According to the city's 25th-anniversary booklet, 15 of Greenbelt's "boys gave the supreme sacrifice." As the pressures of war eased, Greenbelt expanded even more. New, freestanding homes, larger than most of Greenbelt's government-built homes, would be erected in and around the original town, and what was originally a veterans' organization eventually organized a cooperative to buy the town from the federal government in 1952.

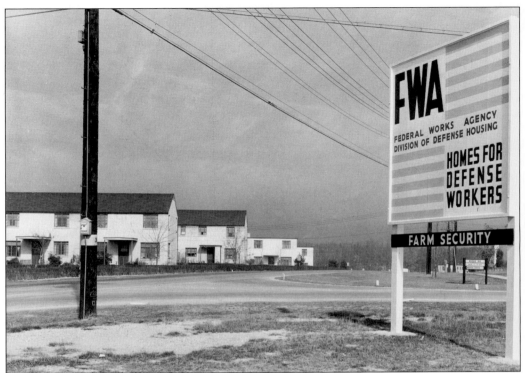

In 1941, Farm Security Administration (FSA) photographers returned to Greenbelt to photograph the expansion of the town. This sign announces the Federal Works Agency project. Greenbelt's frame homes were one of 43 such housing projects throughout the country and are still sometimes referred to in Greenbelt as defense homes or frame homes. (Courtesy Library of Congress, photograph by Arthur Rothstein.)

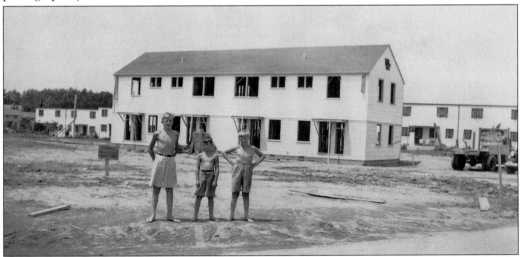

Many Greenbelt pioneer children recall playing at the construction site where 1,000 additional temporary homes were added to Greenbelt beginning in 1941 to house war workers and those on active duty. In the photograph above, young men of the McCarl family pose in front of the construction. These wood-frame homes were never demolished and are still occupied today. (Courtesy Greenbelt Museum.)

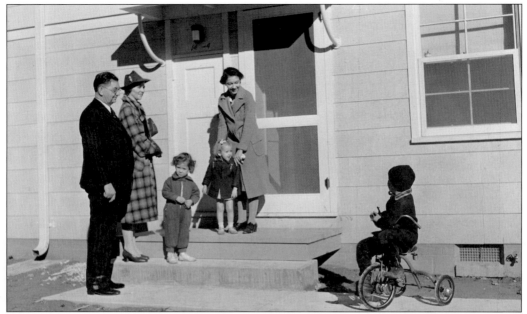

A caption on the back of this photograph reads, "Greenbelt, MD. December 1941. Mrs. S. Hartford Downs, who has been a resident of Greenbelt for 3 years, and Mayor Allen D. Morrison, welcome one of the first residents of the new defense homes at Greenbelt. The new tenant, Mrs. Lloyd Eschenauer, is shown with her young daughter. Her husband is an aircraft painter at Bolling Field. They came to Greenbelt from Pennsylvania." (Courtesy Library of Congress, photograph by Arthur Rothstein.)

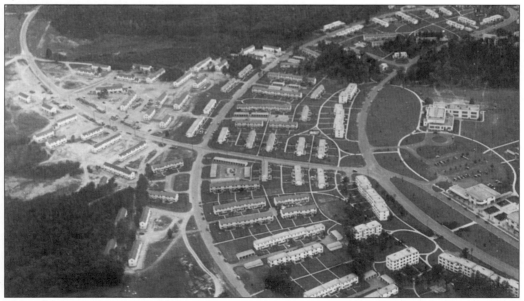

This aerial view shows the additional housing constructed at Greenbelt. Though the superblock plan was utilized in the new areas, some observers were critical of the hurried construction. A lack of landscaping left many yards muddy, leading to the nickname "Mudbelt." In total, the government built an additional 148 one-bedroom apartments, 602 two-bedroom row houses, and 250 three-bedroom row houses. (Courtesy Greenbelt Museum.)

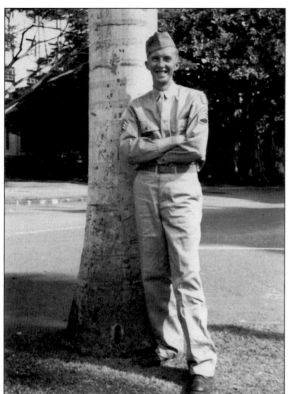

As Greenbelt's young men went off to war, life continued in Greenbelt. S.Sgt. Harry L. Bell Jr. of Ridge Road is pictured here in his uniform. He would tragically be one of the 15 young men from the town to be killed during World War II. (Courtesy Greenbelt Museum.)

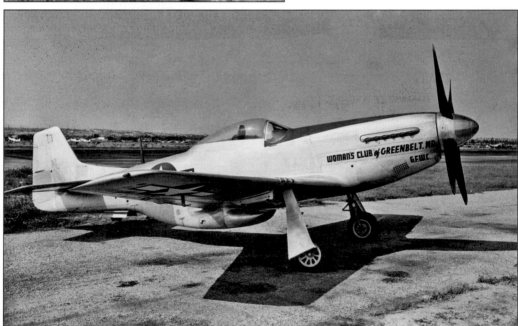

The Woman's Club of Greenbelt was honored in April 1943 by having its name painted on an active North American P-51 Mustang fighter plane. The General Federation of Woman's Clubs, which raised money for bombers and fighter planes in World War II, selected names of its most active chapters for this award. (Courtesy Greenbelt Museum.)

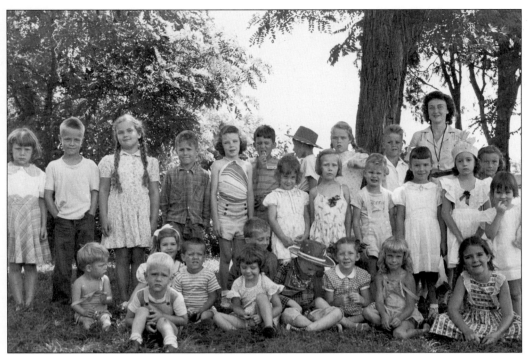

During Word War II, Prince George's County funded the training of high school girls to supervise playgrounds in various communities. Marion Benson Hastings, a Greenbelt pioneer child, was one of these supervisors. This photograph shows her and the Greenbelt children she looked after. (Courtesy Greenbelt Museum.)

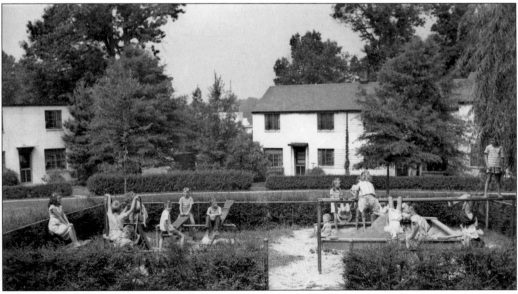

Greenbelt had three times the birthrate of the rest of the country. Once these children entered school, there was not enough space to accommodate them. Double shifts were necessary at both the high school and Center School. By 1943, there were three shifts of Greenbelt kindergartners. (Courtesy Tugwell Room, Greenbelt branch of Prince George's County Memorial Library.)

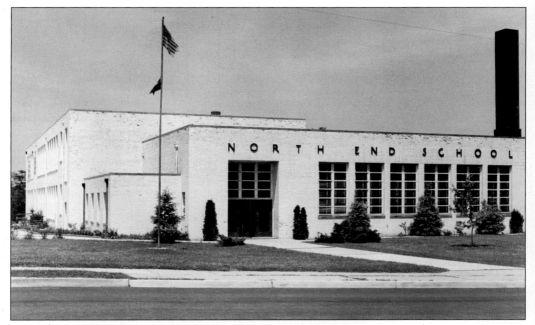

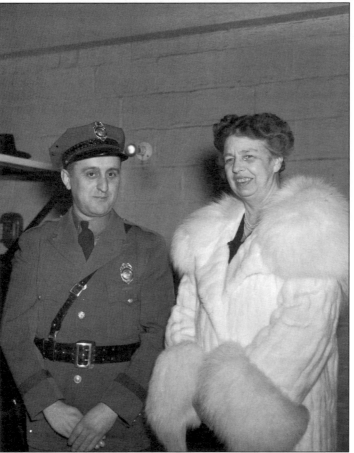

Due to the enormous number of children in Greenbelt and the addition of the defense homes, an additional school, North End Elementary, was built. It was completed in May 1945. In 1992, the school was torn down and replaced by a new Greenbelt Elementary School. (Courtesy Greenbelt Museum.)

On February 21, 1942, the first lady spoke at a defense rally held by the Greenbelt Defense Corps in order to raise funds for medical equipment and supplies. Eleanor Roosevelt was photographed here with town policeman George Panagoulis. (Courtesy Greenbelt Museum.)

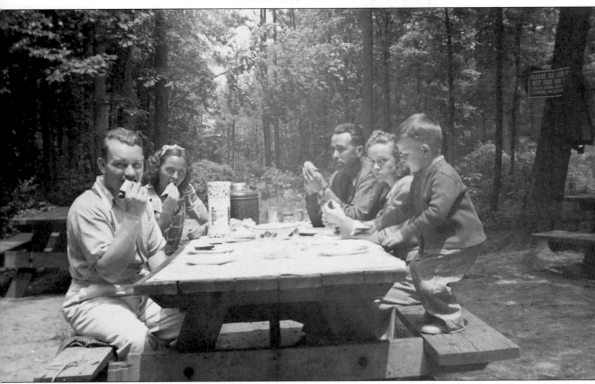

Indian Springs was an area in Greenbelt much beloved by residents. The name references some of the last Native American tribes to inhabit the Greenbelt area: the Senecas and Sinnehannas. The land was also owned by the Walker family from the late 18th century to the 20th. Isaac Walker was a lieutenant in the Revolutionary War. In this photograph, the Frank family enjoys a picnic lunch in the summer of 1941. Pictured from left to right are John Frank, Edith Frank, John W. Biggers, Blanche (Murray) Baldwin, and a young John Ray Frank. Greenbelt pioneer Louise Steinle Winker also frequently visited the area. She described it this way in an oral history: "There was a path over the dam and through the woods to Indian Springs which was a cool and beautiful spot. There were seats around some of the big trees and picnic tables and springs of the coolest, clearest water you can imagine. In the summer, some of us kids would pack up our lunches and hike to Indian Springs." (Courtesy John Ray Frank.)

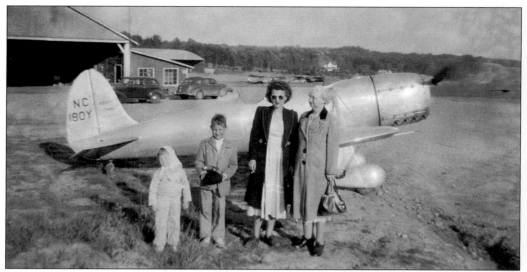

Frederick "Fritz" Schrom built an airport on his family's farm, which was located just east of Greenbelt, in 1928. The Civilian Pilot Training Program used the field actively in the late 1930s to train student pilots, many of whom were from the University of Maryland. By 1940, over 50 planes utilized the field, and 120 pilots, mechanics, and instructors flew, worked, and trained there. The airport closed briefly during the war. In 1944, it reopened to serve as a training center for the Civil Air Patrol. Fritz Schrom's wife ran the airport while her husband finished his military service. The 2,000–3,000-foot grass runway, eventually paved in 1949, was located just north of what is now Hanover Parkway; a city park is located there today. The runway ended on land that became the Baltimore-Washington Parkway in 1954. Children from the area loved to visit the airport and were often photographed standing near planes. Above, Easter Desque poses with her mother and two children from nearby Mount Rainier, Maryland, and below, John Ray Frank (top right) and friends explore a plane at the airport. (Above, courtesy Greenbelt Museum; below, courtesy John Ray Frank.)

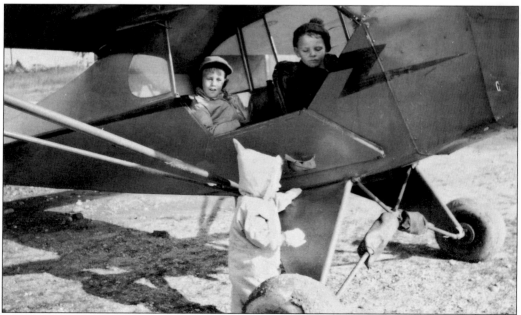

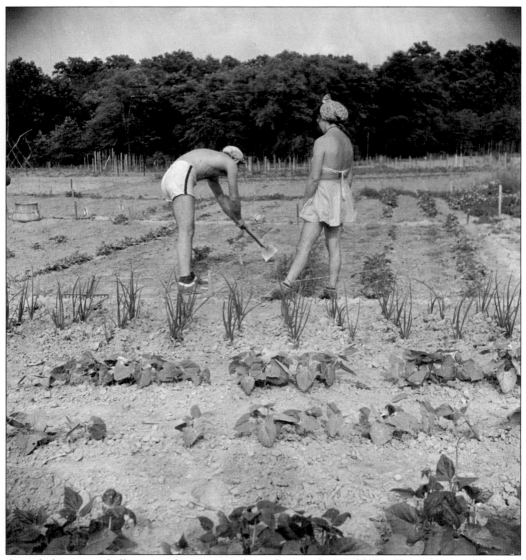

Greenbelt's original allotment plots were ready-made areas for World War II–era Victory Gardens. The town newspaper estimated that over 350 had been planted by 1943. Many residents remember gardening during wartime. Greenbelter Garnett Megee recalled, "When our second child was born we moved from our Parkway apartment to 2-A Southway and lived there until I was drafted in World War II. It seemed that life really burst into bloom here. . . . Also the town plowed up some adjacent fields and gave anyone who desired a Victory Garden, 50 foot by 50 foot. This was a wonderful hobby and we had much pleasure with our garden." (Courtesy Library of Congress, photograph by Marjory Collins.)

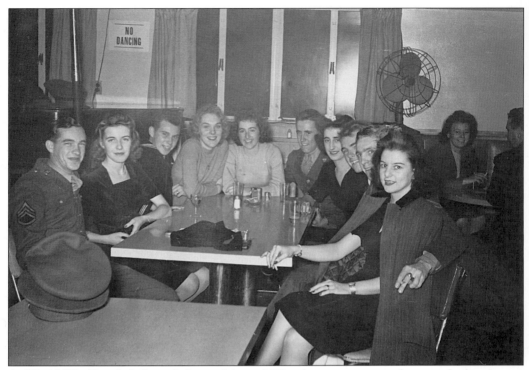

As World War II ended, Greenbelters celebrated. This festive group was photographed in August 1945 at Waldrup's restaurant in nearby Brentwood, Maryland. Pictured are, from left to right, Dick Bates, Dotty Herbert, George Davidsen, Helen Goetzger, unidentified, Bob Sommers, Jerry Andrus, Mike Loftus, Jack Gale, and June Donoghue. (Courtesy Greenbelt Museum.)

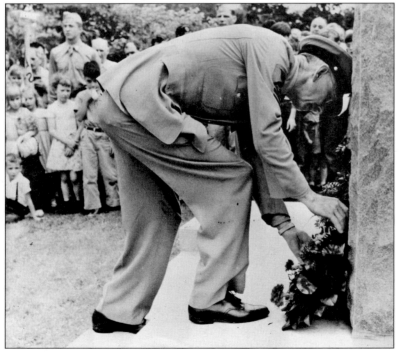

In the photograph at left, Harry L. "Pop" Bell places a wreath on Greenbelt's war memorial. His son, Harry L. Bell Jr., was killed in World War II. (Courtesy Greenbelt Museum.)

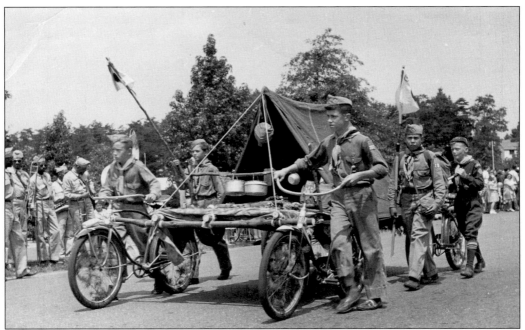

Greenbelt continued to celebrate holidays with parades as the war ended. Note the African American service members standing beyond the Boy Scouts in the photograph above. The photograph below depicts a young lady liberty. (Above, courtesy John Maffay; below, courtesy Greenbelt Museum.)

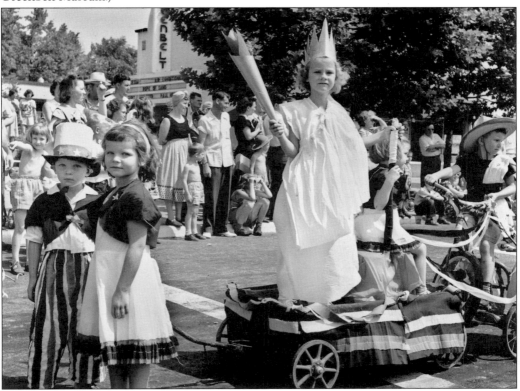

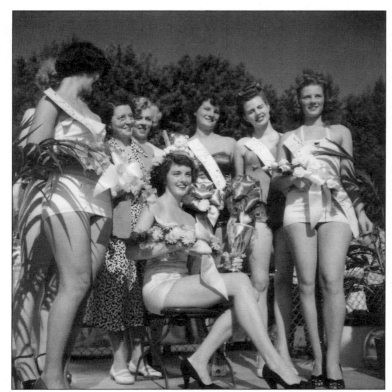

With the war over, Greenbelters got back to the serious business of having fun. The young ladies who competed for the title of Miss Greenbelt pose at the pool in this c. 1949 image along with then-mayor Elizabeth Harrington. Each young woman was sponsored by a local business, and for many years, the Miss Greenbelt competition was decided by citizens dropping coins into jars located around town. (Courtesy Greenbelt Museum, photograph by Paul Kasko.)

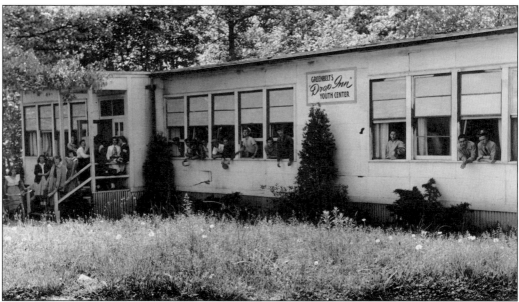

The Drop Inn, the town's youth center, offered Greenbelt's teenagers a place to hang out. It was originally housed in the Athletic Club building, then beneath the firehouse–police station in 1944, but its 200 members outgrew the space. The community raised $5,000 for a new building, which opened May 1947 and featured a library, snack bar, game room, and lounge. It was largely run by the teens themselves under the supervision of Eileen Labukas of the Greenbelt Recreation Department. (Courtesy Greenbelt Museum, photograph by Paul Kasko.)

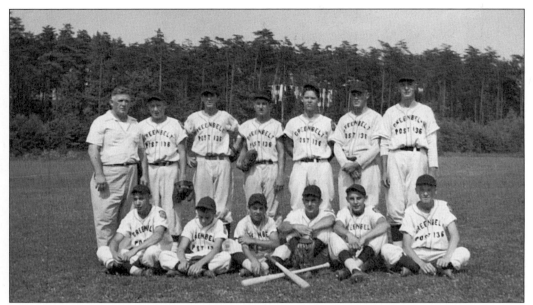

Baseball, important from the beginning of the town, continued to be a popular sport. The American Legion Post No. 136 team from 1947 ended the season with 32 wins and 5 losses. Pictured are, from left to right, (first row) Jacob Hammond, Ralph Longnecker, Rube Randolph, Harry Benefiel, Ronald Bierwagon, and Gladstone Lewis; (second row) coach Leo Mullins, Lester Sander Jr., Bobo Hawes, Harry Randolph, George Bauer, John Martone, and Robert Scott. (Courtesy Greenbelt Museum.)

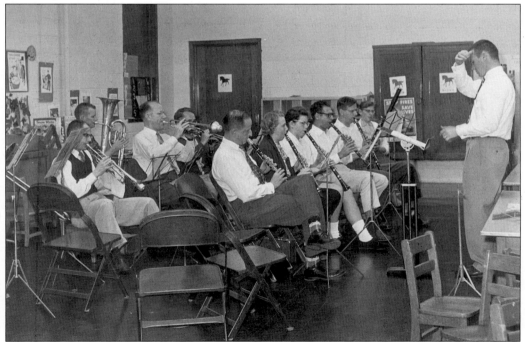

The Greenbelt Community Band, pictured here in 1947, was originally formed in 1940 and is still an active organization in Greenbelt that performs several times a year. (Courtesy Greenbelt Museum, photograph by Paul Kasko.)

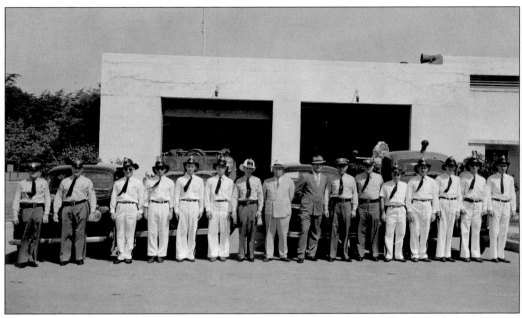

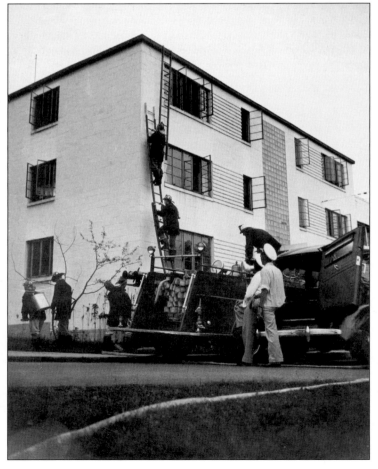

The Greenbelt Fire Department, along with the police department, was originally established by the FSA. Police and fire department members pose above with town manager James T. Gobbel (eighth from left) and Mayor George Bauer (ninth from left) in 1946. At left, the fire department practices a rescue in 1946. Today, the fire department is involved in one of Greenbelt's beloved traditions when an engine delivers Santa to the annual holiday tree lighting. (Above, courtesy Greenbelt Museum; left, courtesy Tugwell Room, Greenbelt branch of the Prince George's County Memorial Library.)

The Mother and Child sculpture by Lenore Thomas, the artist who also sculpted the bas-reliefs on the elementary school, originally had a drinking fountain at its base. Though not always popular with the townspeople, the sculpture anchors the center of town. In this photograph taken on Memorial Day, 1942, a flag waves in the foreground. (Courtesy Library of Congress, photograph by Marjory Collins.)

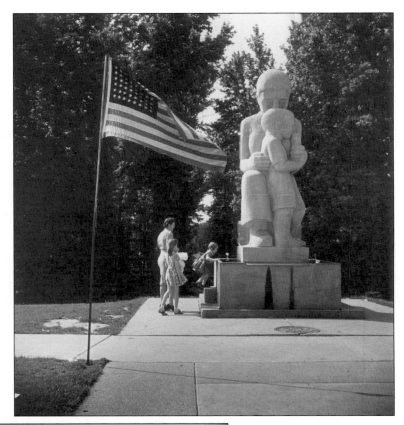

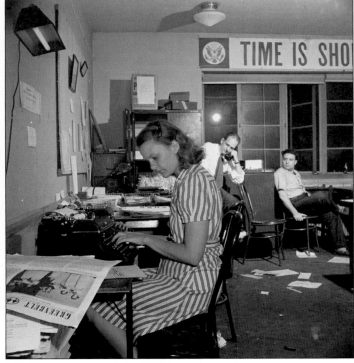

The community's newspaper, the *Cooperator*, continued through the 1940s and, following the war, was an important source of information regarding the sale of the town by the federal government. (Courtesy Library of Congress, photograph by Marjory Collins.)

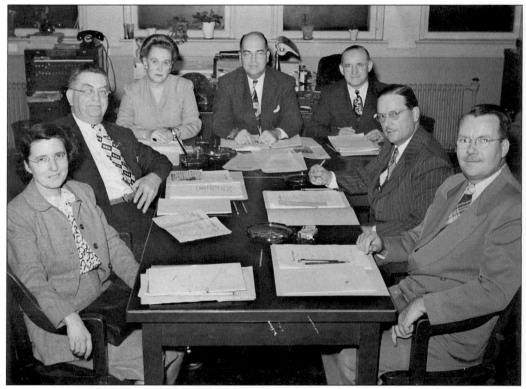

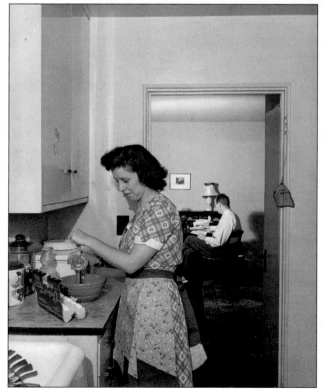

Greenbelt's first female mayor, Elizabeth Harrington (front left), pictured here with the city council, was elected in 1949, but she was not the first woman to be elected to the town council; that distinction belonged to Ruth Taylor, who had been elected to council in 1938. Taylor was the first woman elected to any governing body in the history of Prince George's County. (Courtesy Greenbelt Museum.)

Despite women having joined the workforce in large numbers during wartime, photographs like this one from 1946 depict some women's return to domesticity in Greenbelt. (Courtesy Library of Congress, photograph by Gretchen Van Tassel.)

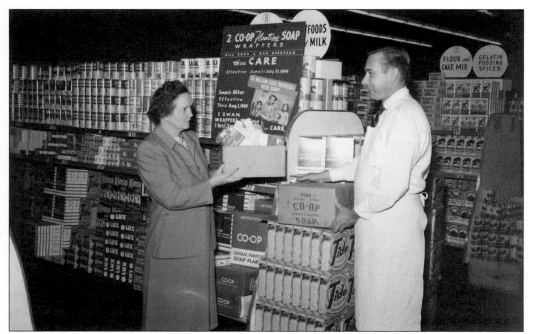

Greenbelters did their best with wartime rationing and continued to patronize the co-op food store. Here a soap offer is being advertised, "2 Co-op Floating Soap wrappers will send a bar overseas thru C.A.R.E. 30 Million kids overseas need soap!" (Courtesy Greenbelt Museum, photograph by Paul Kasko.)

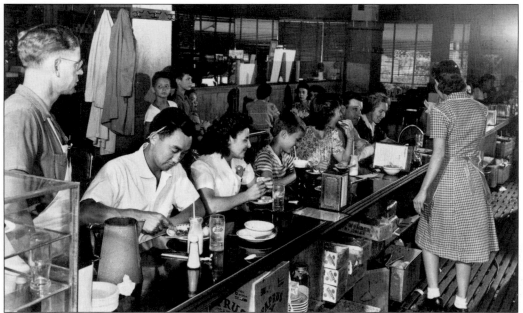

The soda fountain would eventually be replaced by a High's Dairy Store, but following the war, it continued to draw steady business. References in the town newspaper indicate that African Americans were served at the lunch counter as early as 1939, which was unusual for the region because of segregation. It was reported that those objecting to this practice were shouted down at citizens association meetings. (Courtesy Library of Congress.)

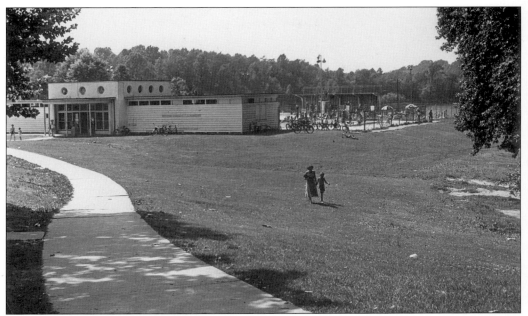

The Greenbelt pool continued to be a popular recreation spot for residents, and Greenbelt's green spaces were very much enjoyed. (Courtesy Greenbelt Museum.)

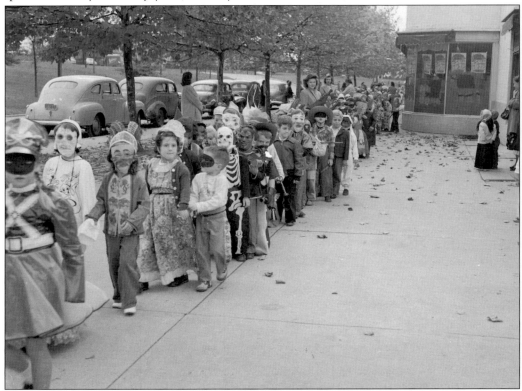

The annual Halloween parade is another long-standing tradition in Greenbelt. This photograph shows a number of children participating in the late 1940s. (Courtesy Greenbelt Museum, photograph by Paul Kasko.)

Five

A COOPERATIVE
BUYS THE TOWN

Greenbelt changed significantly in the 1950s. Following the end of World War II, as the federal government discussed selling the greenbelt towns, citizens began organizing to buy it. In 1952, they succeeded, and the original housing was purchased by a cooperative, Greenbelt Veterans Housing Corporation. The same cooperative exists today, though its name has changed to Greenbelt Homes, Inc. The additional wartime homes added in the 1940s, coupled with the postwar baby boom, resulted in many more children in Greenbelt than had been present even in the first years of the town. They went to school and enjoyed the playgrounds and open green spaces in and around Greenbelt with the same enthusiasm as their earlier counterparts.

The adults in Greenbelt continued to organize as they had before. Many of Greenbelt's churches, which had held services in the elementary school or the theater, built dedicated spaces on vacant land. The Greenbelt Community Church, St. Hugh's Catholic Church, Mishkan Torah, Greenbelt Baptist Church, Holy Cross Lutheran, and Mowatt Memorial United Methodist Church all erected buildings in the 1950s. Construction of new housing also began to take place. The Lakeside development began in 1953 as a cooperative land-purchase venture in the Greenbelt tradition, and the first of 65 freestanding single-family homes was built by 1954. Beginning in 1956, homes were constructed in the Woodland Hills subdivision, also on a cooperative basis, and in 1959, private builders began to construct the Lakewood subdivision. As families grew and more options became available, many families moved from Greenbelt's original housing into larger single-family homes, beginning a tradition that would continue in the 1960s and 1970s.

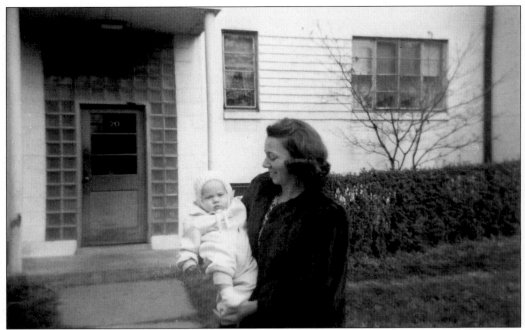

Eileen Labukas stands holding infant daughter Kathy Labukas in front of the Greenbelt apartment building where the family lived around 1950. The Labukas family would move from their apartment to a freestanding home in Lakeside in the 1950s, a trend that many Greenbelt families followed. (Courtesy Kathy Labukas.)

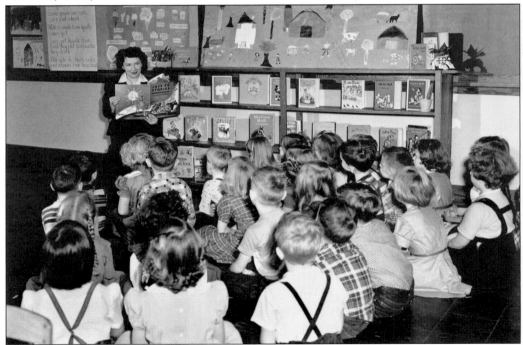

The baby boom hit Greenbelt, as well as the nation, in the postwar era. In this photograph, children have gathered in the library within Center School in 1953 to hear Rudyard Kipling's *Just So Stories* at a story hour. (Courtesy Greenbelt Museum, photograph by Paul Kasko.)

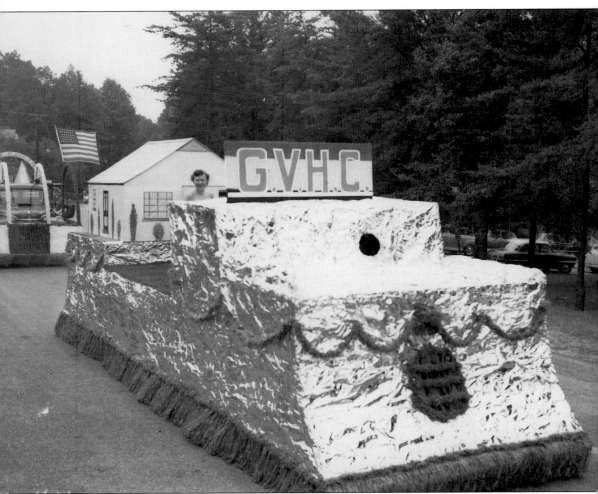

In 1947, hundreds of residents created the Greenbelt Mutual Home Owners Corporation (GMHOC), a nonprofit corporation formed for the purpose of purchasing the entire town of Greenbelt and its surrounding land. The GMHOC reconstituted itself as the Greenbelt Veterans Housing Corporation (GVHC) in 1949 in order to comply with a federal law that the government first offer to sell the town's housing and land to a group of potential residents, half of whom needed to be veterans. (Courtesy Greenbelt Museum, photograph by Paul Kasko.)

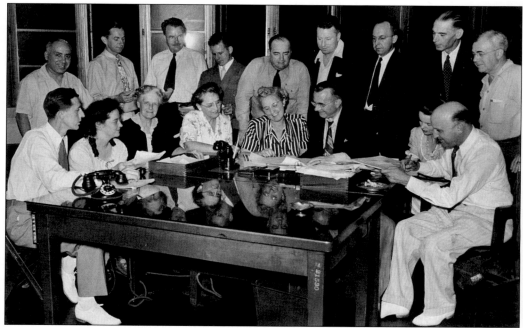

In December 1952, the government sold 1,572 housing units, which excluded the apartment buildings and the commercial buildings and included only 708 acres of land, for $6,995,669 to GVHC, while the apartment and commercial buildings were sold to six other private purchasers. GVHC sold much of Greenbelt's land to developers, who built detached single-family homes and apartments. Greenbelt's sale was one of the most contentious moments in the town's history, because many tenants preferred to rent rather than buy into the cooperative. Thus, many residents moved out of Greenbelt after the sale. In the photograph above, papers are signed, making the sale official. Below, Mr. Hansen became the first official resident to place a deposit for a Greenbelt home in April 1952. Florence Shinderman (center) and Marie Thomas are also pictured. (Both, courtesy Greenbelt Museum, photographs by Hans Jorgensen.)

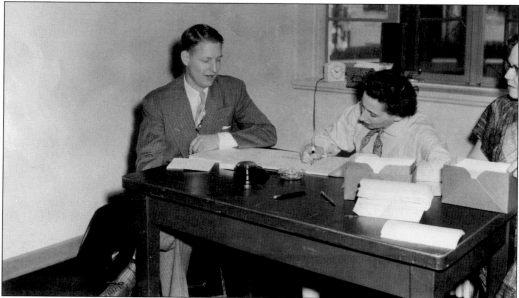

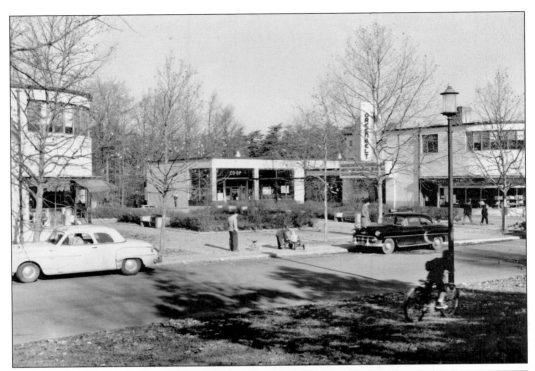

In 1954, the US government sold the center commercial buildings to a private real estate firm, and in 1956, the cooperative stores, except for the grocery store, vacated. A Ben Franklin five-and-dime store opened on June 7, 1957, replacing the co-op variety store, and it remained open for 30 years. (Both, courtesy Greenbelt Museum, photographs by Paul Kasko.)

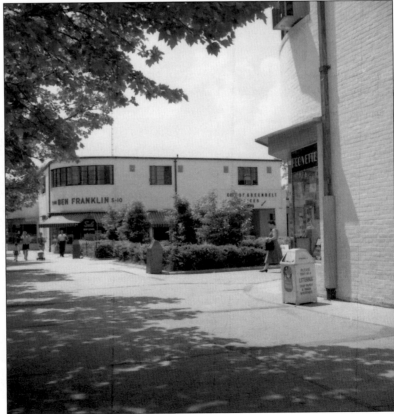

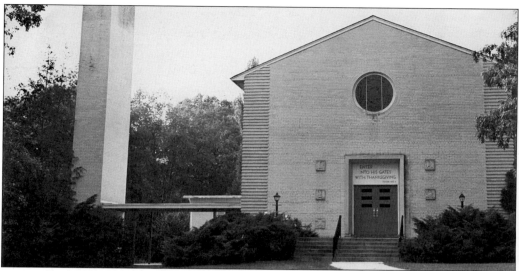

Protestant church services had been held for many years in Center School, which doubled as a community center. The Greenbelt Community Church (above) opened in June 1950. There is a long history of Greenbelt's churches cooperating with one another, and according to an article in the *Washington Post* that covered the first service held there, the Jewish Community Center of Greenbelt presented the church with the gift of a lectern. Ben and Ethel Rosenzweig, pictured below in 1957, were a Greenbelt pioneer family who, along with several other Jewish pioneer families, began the Greenbelt Hebrew Congregation in the first few years of the community. Services began in 1939 in Center School. In the early 1950s, construction of the Mishkan Torah sanctuary began. Joe Dalis remembers the construction this way: "Unexpected help came from the community as word spread about the efforts of do-it-yourselfers to erect a synagogue. So in their spare time Catholics, Protestants and others sweated alongside our members, all working to build a House of God. At long last, their labors were rewarded when our synagogue was dedicated on March 20, 1955, with appropriate ceremonies." (Above, courtesy *Greenbelt News Review*; below, courtesy Richard Rosenzweig.)

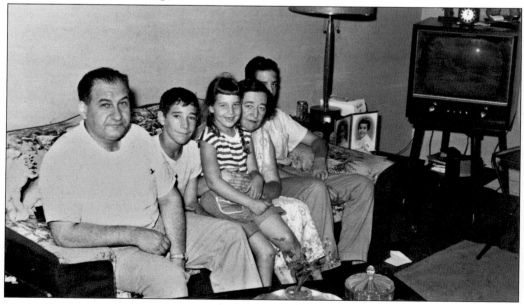

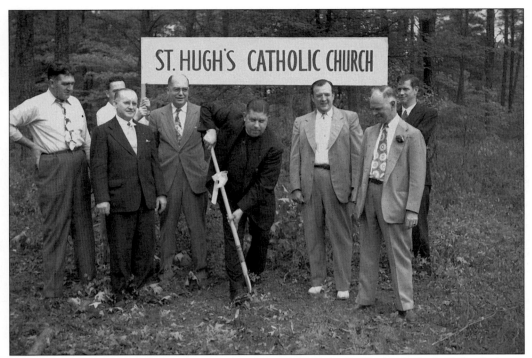

Rev. Father Victor Dowgiallo breaks ground on May 15, 1949, for St. Hugh's Catholic School; classes began the following October. The parish had been founded in 1947. The school closed in June 2010 due to declining enrollment. (Courtesy Greenbelt Museum, photograph by Paul Kasko.)

This photograph depicts the ground-breaking for Holy Cross Lutheran Church, which was dedicated in July 1952. Lutheran services had first been held in 1944 in the home of Greenbelters Adele and Edward Trumbule. Later, they were held in the Center School. (Courtesy Greenbelt Museum, photograph by Paul Kasko.)

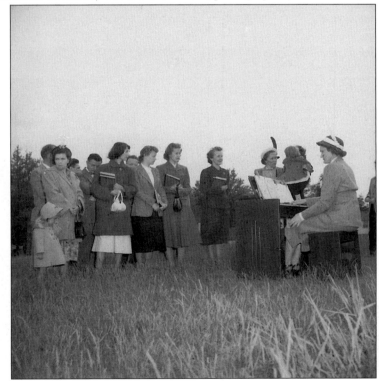

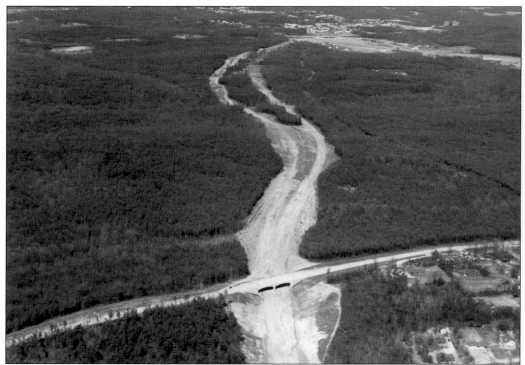

Plans for a highway between Washington and Baltimore had been discussed for several decades, as busy US Route 1 had a high accident rate and there were several federal entities that would be served by the highway, including Fort Meade. Construction began in 1947, and the parkway opened to traffic in stages between 1950 and 1954. (Courtesy Greenbelt Museum, photograph by Paul Kasko.)

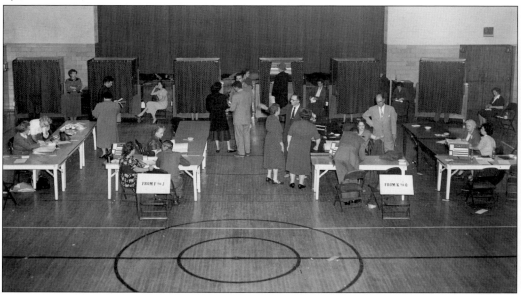

Civic engagement continued to be important in Greenbelt in the 1950s. Elections were held in the gym in the elementary school. This photograph depicts the city election of 1953. (Courtesy Greenbelt Museum, photograph by Paul Kasko.)

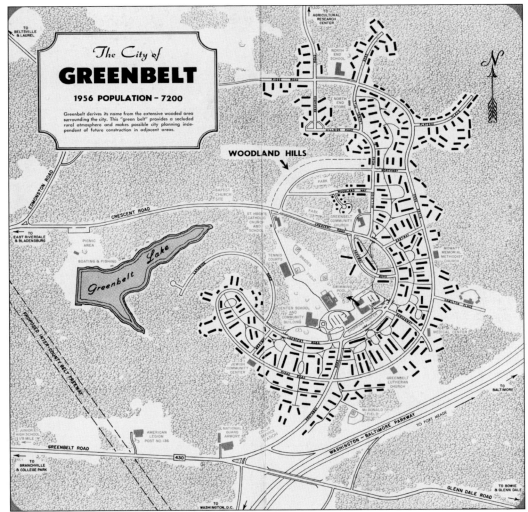

A 1956 brochure for Woodland Hills written by Woodway Community Development, Inc., addresses future home builders directly by stating, "Here is your opportunity to acquire ownership of your future home site in the beautiful, residential subdivision of Woodland Hills, Greenbelt, Maryland." It goes on to describe that the Woodland Hills development consists of 49 lots, averaging 10,000 square feet at 75 by 140 feet, and that prices range from $2,900 to $3,390 for corner lots. It also lists Greenbelt's impressive education and recreation resources: "Recreation Department, Youth Center, 18 'tot' playgrounds, indoor roller skating, 3 large playgrounds, swimming pool, swimming instruction, wading pool, 4 tennis courts, 2 handball courts, 3 hardball diamonds, 1 softball diamond (illuminated night games), 2 football fields, 1 basketball court, 10 bowling alleys, lake for fishing and boating." It adds, "This residential development has been organized as a non-profit corporation by a group of outstanding Greenbelt residents." (Courtesy Greenbelt Museum.)

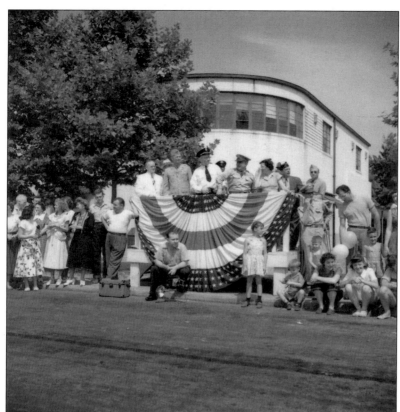

Some of Greenbelt's traditions, begun in the late 1930s and interrupted by the austerity of wartime, were celebrated again in the 1950s. The Labor Day Festival, officially established in 1955, is still an important tradition in Greenbelt and one that brings out residents and visitors alike. The parade still attracts large numbers of spectators. Memorial Day parades (below) were also popular. (Both, courtesy Greenbelt Museum, photographs by Paul Kasko.)

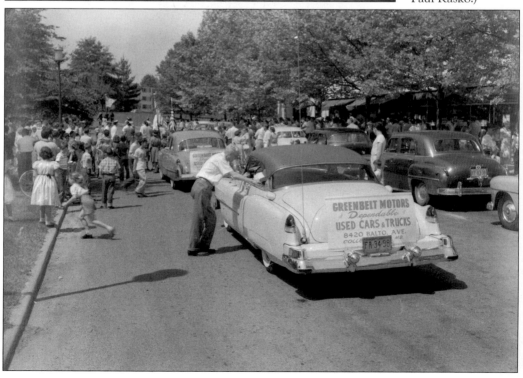

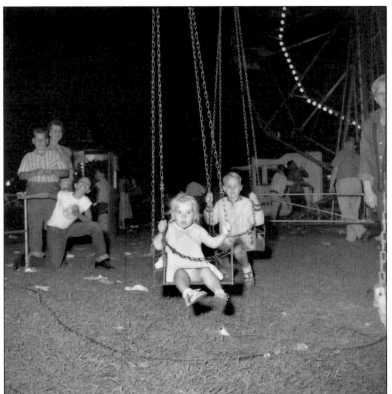

Midway rides are still installed in Greenbelt's historical area over Labor Day weekend, and community groups sponsor booths and food vendors as they did in the 1950s. (Both, courtesy Greenbelt Museum, photographs by Paul Kasko.)

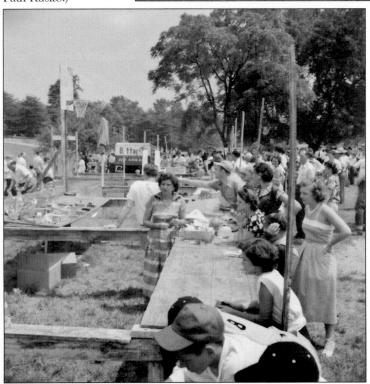

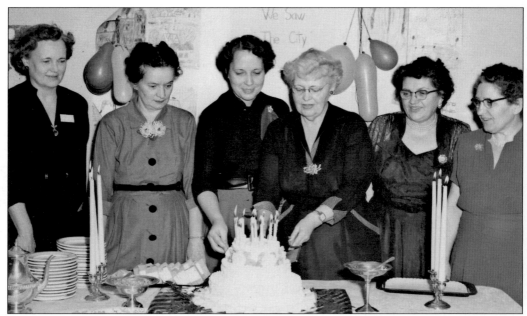

The Woman's Club, established in 1939, was an important organization in Greenbelt until it disbanded in 1990. Over the years, members supported the formation of the Drop Inn and the Youth Center and participated in USO and Red Cross activities during the war. Attending this Woman's Club birthday party were, from left to right, Mrs. Charles McDonald, Mrs. James Smith, Mrs. Mott, Mrs. Thomas Freeman, Mrs. Charles Cormack, and Elizabeth Turner. (Courtesy Greenbelt Museum, photograph by Paul Kasko.)

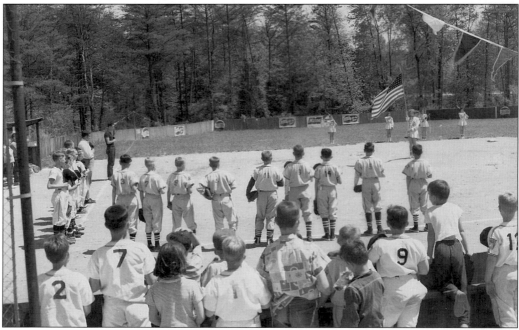

Baseball was a beloved sport in Greenbelt from the beginning. Soon after the town was populated, leagues formed around the housing courts and through American Legion Post No. 136. This scene depicts opening day in 1955. (Courtesy Greenbelt Museum, photograph by Paul Kasko.)

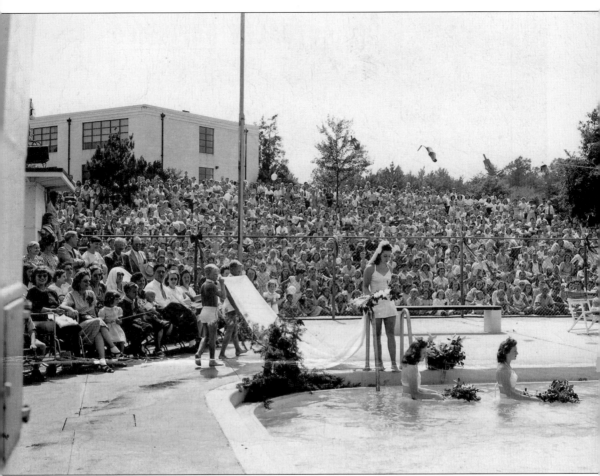

For many years, water pageants took place at the swimming pool, such as the one above, which featured a mock wedding. They were produced by Eileen Labukas and Ora Donoghue, recreation department employees, and drew large crowds. Greenbelter June Hammersla Franklin recalls, "Every year over the Labor Day Weekend we had a pool pageant. We had swimming races, diving contests and exhibitions and there was a water ballet. . . . I was one of the mermaids in the ballet. We all wore white caps and black suits and we did all the things Esther Williams used to do." (Courtesy Kathy Labukas.)

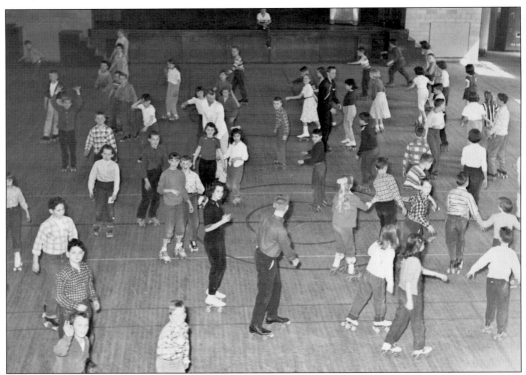

Many Greenbelters have fond memories of roller-skating around town and, on certain occasions, in the school gymnasium. (Courtesy Greenbelt Museum, photograph by Paul Kasko.)

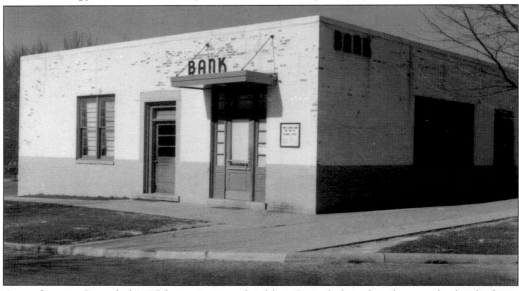

According to Greenbelt's 25th-anniversary booklet, Greenbelters lined up at the bank above on April 18, 1952, to make initial payments as members of the housing cooperative. In 1957, residents organized to form an additional cooperative, the Twin Pines Savings and Loan, whose purpose was to "promote thrift and make loans on co-op homes." Rexford Guy Tugwell, who lived in Greenbelt briefly in the late 1950s, was one of the initial members of the board of directors. (Courtesy Greenbelt Museum, photograph by Paul Kasko.)

Six

GREENBELT EXPANDS IN THE 1960S AND 1970S

Greenbelt continued to grow in the 1960s and 1970s, though residents fought to shape that growth by protesting against high-density housing and excessive commercial development. The construction of new housing, begun in the previous decade, continued. Springhill Lake, reportedly one of the largest planned garden apartment complexes on the east coast, began renting to tenants in 1963. Its garden apartments, situated on green space with a system of interior walkways, reflected, to some degree, Greenbelt's original plan, as would many of the other developments constructed. Lakeside North and Charlestowne Village, apartment and townhouse developments, came along in 1964, and by 1966, more new housing was also being built in Lakecrest and Boxwood Village. According to a handbook distributed to residents, "Today, development plans are being proposed for almost every parcel of open land located within the city and nearby. At the same time, the city is making every effort to assure the orderly growth of these lands and to provide for the needs of a growing community." In 1963, there were 23 playgrounds with 106 acres of city parkland, not including Greenbelt Park, an 11,000-acre federal park also within the city.

Residents responded to growth in the 1960s and 1970s as they had since the town's founding by becoming activists, forming committees, and working toward change. Many families wanted to move out of the smaller original housing but did not want to leave the quality of life that Greenbelt offered, so they moved within the community. One major incident that brought residents together was a court case in which an area developer, Charles Bresler, filed a $2-million libel suit against the *Greenbelt News Review* and its president at the time, Alfred M. Skolnik. The community rallied around the paper and the accused and contributed around $30,000 to the defense. The case was finally decided by the Supreme Court, and the *News Review* won, which many saw as a decision that reaffirmed the freedom of the press. The construction of the Beltway also had a major impact on the area, and as a result, the 1970s witnessed increased commercial development.

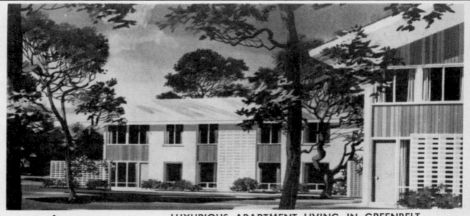

LUXURIOUS APARTMENT LIVING IN GREENBELT
A COMPLETELY PLANNED COMMUNITY FOR 5000 PEOPLE

Introducing

Springhill Lake

Imagine having the recreational facilities of a country club right at your doorstep—several swimming pools, bath house and lounge area, equipped play areas, community house with a dance deck overlooking a lake, golf course, nursery school and many other facilities. Air conditioned garden apartments and townhouses provide huge closets, color kitchens with eating space, and window walls that look onto your private patio or balcony. Truly luxury—but at reasonable rentals. Mid-winter occupancy. We welcome inquiries. Phone FE 8-6809.

Builders & Developers
of award-winning
communities

1730 K St., N.W.
Washington, D.C.

When it opened in 1963, the Springhill Lake garden apartment complex was one of the largest on the east coast. This 1962 advertisement references Greenbelt's history: "Introducing Springhill Lake, Luxurious Apartment Living in Greenbelt, a completely planned community for 5000 people." (Courtesy Greenbelt Museum.)

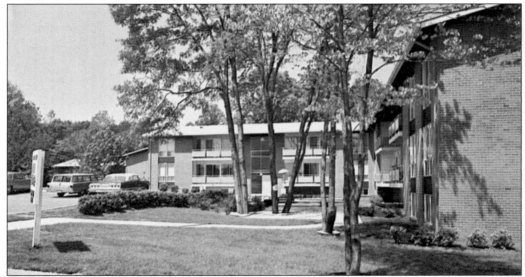

Because the complex was so large, it took seven years to complete the nearly 2,900 low-rise apartment and townhouse units that make up the Springhill Lake development, the name of which was changed several times over the years. It was designed by well-known architects Cohen Haft and Associates. Once occupied, the complex's 10,000 residents more than doubled Greenbelt's population, which grew from 7,480 in 1960 to 18,199 in 1970. (Courtesy Greenbelt Museum.)

The Cooley family moved in to the Springhill Lake apartment complex soon after it opened. Brenda Cooley remembers that "there was a pool, a lake, plenty of green space and our apartment was very nice and was air conditioned which was unusual at the time. It felt quite luxurious. You could walk to the grocery store and pharmacy and I remember taking a Chinese cooking class there. My husband, Jim Cooley, worked not far away at NASA. It was a one bedroom apartment so we moved to Boxwood Village a few years after our daughter was born." Debbie Cooley, right, poses in front of the Springhill Lake apartments in 1967. Like many families, the Cooleys moved for more living space but stayed within Greenbelt. Below, Debbie and Brenda Cooley stand in front of their home in Boxwood Village with Ed Cooley, Brenda's father-in-law and Debbie's grandfather. (Both, courtesy Brenda Cooley.)

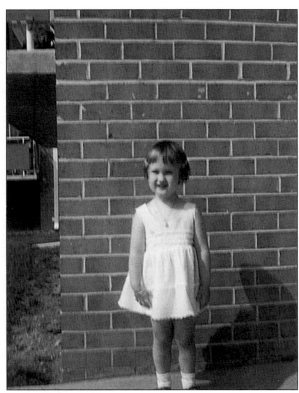

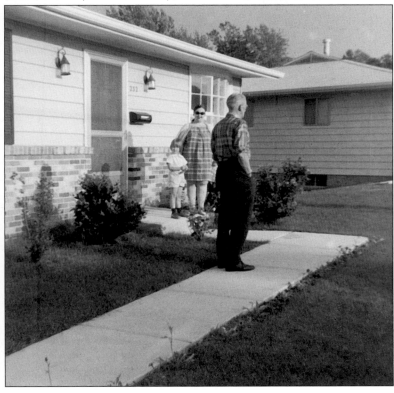

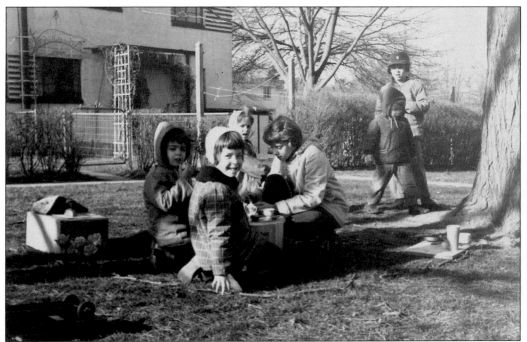

In the photograph above, taken in March 1962, members of the Maffay family enjoy a picnic in the yard outside of their original Greenbelt home. John Maffay, a Greenbelt pioneer child, grew up in the historical part of town and began to raise his family there before he and his wife, Elizabeth, bought a lot and had a larger single-family home built on Northway in the Woodland Hills area of Greenbelt, as many other Greenbelt families would do. Elizabeth Maffay served on Greenbelt's city council from 1969 until 1973. (Both, courtesy Sheila Maffay-Tuthill.)

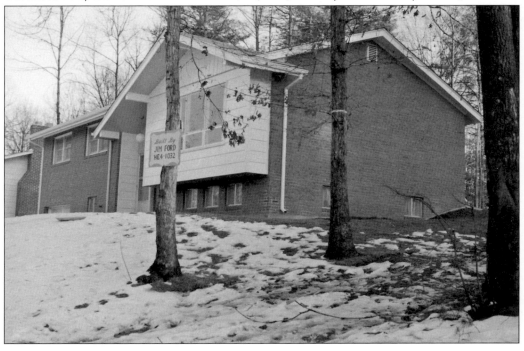

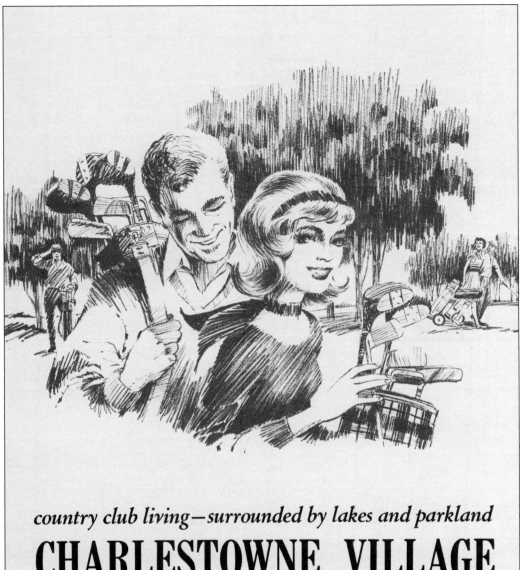

country club living—surrounded by lakes and parkland

CHARLESTOWNE VILLAGE

townhouse apartments in Greenbelt, Maryland

This brochure advertises Charlestowne Village, a townhouse development just west of historic Greenbelt. Text inside reads, "Charlestowne Village, next to the city of Greenbelt, Maryland, is part of a new space age center of apartments, townhouses, shopping and schools. Four minutes from NASA, a minute from a major Capital Beltway cloverleaf at the Baltimore Parkway, it is a short 15 or 20 minutes drive downtown or to Ft. Meade and NSA. In fact, you will be able to drive anywhere in the metropolitan area inside of 25 minutes on the new Beltway without seeing a single traffic light. . . . This is tomorrow's suburban township today, a quiet oasis next to a metropolitan city." (Courtesy Greenbelt Museum.)

Lakeside North was built in 1964 by Rozansky & Kay Construction Co. and designed by architects Herbert H. Johnson and Associates. Its brochure boasts, "Lakeside North is in the center of things just like the old days. Walk along the tree-shaded paths to the village center of Greenbelt. Shop at the supermarket, five and ten, local hardware, gift, drug store or bakery. Buy the latest fashions at Kleins on the square. Go bowling after dinner, or take in a show. Leave the car at home for a change and learn the convenience of living in the center of things." (Courtesy Greenbelt Museum.)

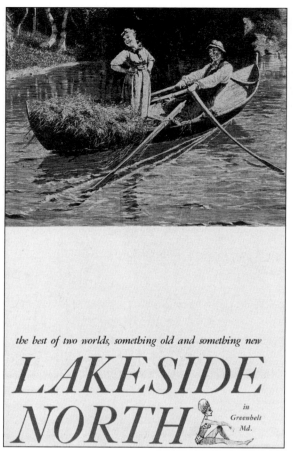

the best of two worlds, something old and something new

LAKESIDE NORTH

in Greenbelt Md.

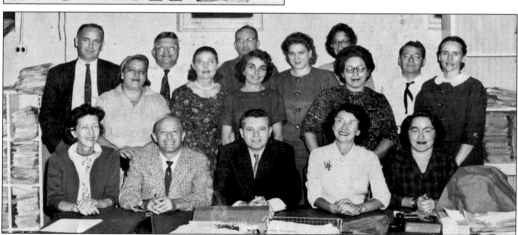

The *News Review* continued to offer a forum where citizens could debate Greenbelt's development. Pictured here is the *News Review* staff at their 15A Parkway offices in 1962. They are, from left to right, (first row) Bess Halperin, Harry Zubkoff, Al Skolnik, Virginia Beauchamp, and Bernice Kastner; (second row) Rita Fisher, Thea Lovell, Elaine Skolnik, Dorothy Sucher, Sid Kastner, and Dorothy White; (back row) Izzy Parker, Vic Fisher, Ross Greenbaum, Margaret Thompson, and Mary Lou Williamson. Volunteers have published the newspaper continuously every week since November 1937 and have never missed an issue. (Courtesy *Greenbelt News Review.*)

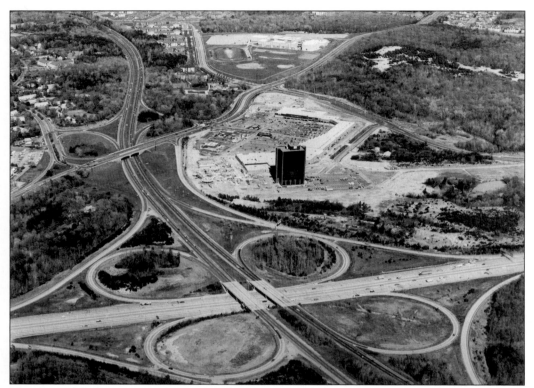

The Capital Beltway opened in 1964, changing Greenbelt's landscape once again. Greenbelt resident Marty Madden recalled construction of the Beltway in 1987: "I remember when the Beltway was built. I remember standing in the middle of that big dirt road during construction wondering how any road could be so big. Dad thought it would be great because you could get up to Montgomery County in less than 20 minutes." (Courtesy *Greenbelt News Review*.)

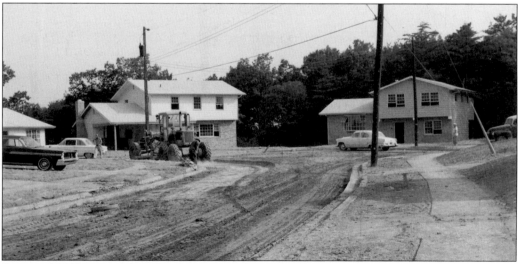

Boxwood Village, another development within Greenbelt's city limits, opened in the spring of 1963. It offered single-family homes that were larger than the town's original New Deal–era dwellings. This photograph shows the development of Julian Court, one of the culs-de-sac built within the development. (Courtesy Greenbelt Museum.)

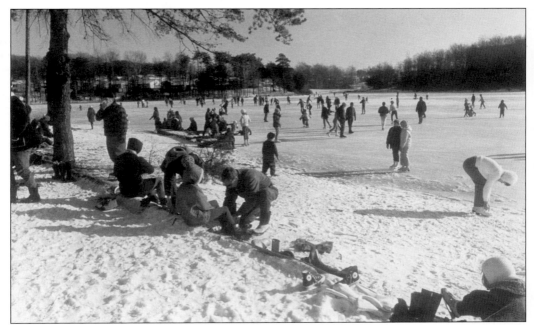

Skating on Greenbelt Lake was a popular winter pastime, and many residents recall the bonfires that were lit on the shore. Unfortunately, the lake has not frozen solid enough in recent years to be skated upon. (Courtesy Greenbelt Museum.)

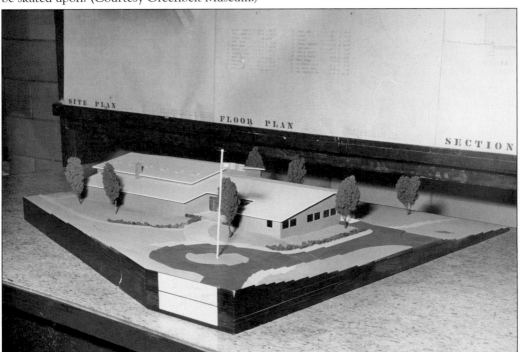

This photograph depicts a scale model of a new youth center, which opened on Labor Day 1961. The new building, with a full-size gym and much more space, replaced the Drop Inn. More recently, a skate park was added to the grounds in front of the building. (Courtesy Greenbelt Museum, photograph by Paul Kasko.)

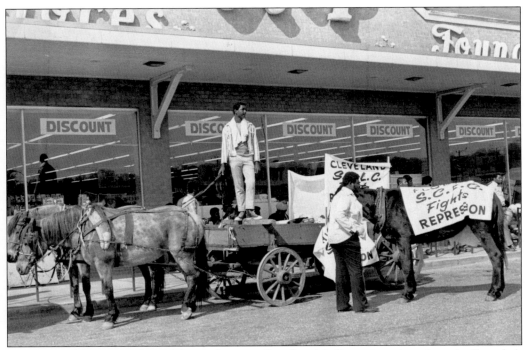

In 1968, roughly 700 members of the northeastern Poor People's Campaign stopped over in Greenbelt on their way to Washington, DC. They stayed at the Community Church and St. Hugh's Catholic Church and were tended to by over 150 volunteers. (Courtesy Greenbelt Museum.)

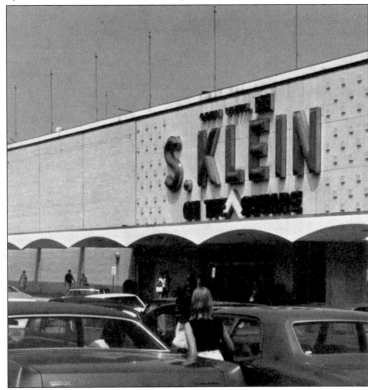

Beltway Plaza was developed by Sidney Brown and First National Realty. It was anchored by the three-story S. Klein department store at one end and an A&P Supermarket in a strip shopping center at the other. There was also a barbershop, single-screen movie theater, and Drug Fair store. According to a *Washington Post* article from July 1962, the 320,000-square-foot S. Klein department store would be the largest department store in the Washington, DC, suburban area. It closed in 1975. (Courtesy Tugwell Room, Greenbelt branch of Prince George's County Memorial Library.)

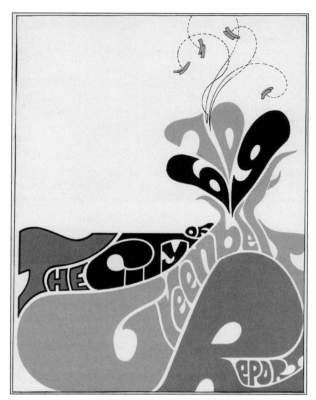

Jack Ballestero designed the cover of the City of Greenbelt's report for 1969–1970. The back cover of the report interprets the exuberant design: "The dynamic growth and development of the city that has occurred is represented by Mr. Ballestero's pop art design of Greenbelt bursting out of the ground and flowering." (Courtesy Greenbelt Museum.)

Greenbelt has had many distinguished visitors over the years. Here, from left to right, Congressman Larry Hogan poses with Patricia Nixon Cox, Greenbelt mayor Richard Pilsky, and city manager James Giese at a 1972 Legacy of Parks ceremony. (Courtesy Greenbelt Museum.)

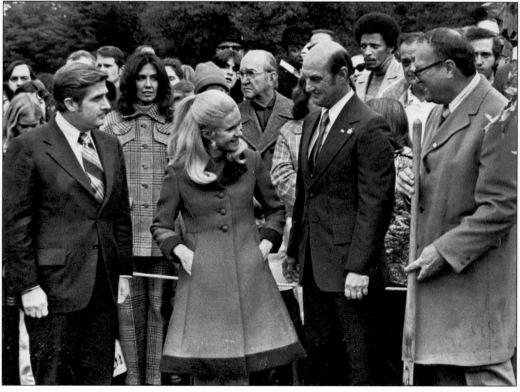

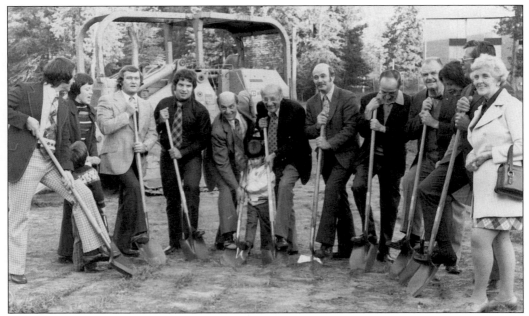

Greenbelt has had a strong commitment to providing recreational facilities and activities for its community members since its creation. With new development in the western part of Greenbelt, the city opened the Springhill Lake Recreation Center in 1975, which, like the Springhill Lake apartment complex, was designed by Cohen Haft and Associates. In this photograph, members of city council along with others break ground for the recreation center. (Courtesy *Greenbelt News Review*.)

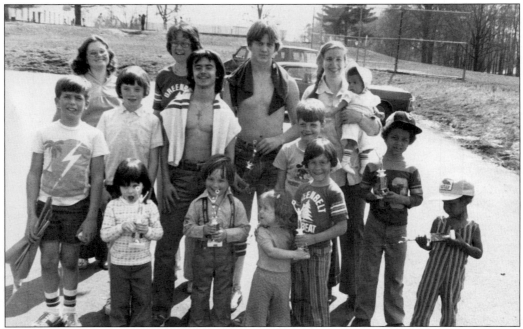

Sports and recreation continued to be an important part of life in Greenbelt for residents of all ages in the 1970s. Pictured above, proud winners of a kite-flying contest show off their trophies. (Courtesy *Greenbelt News Review*.)

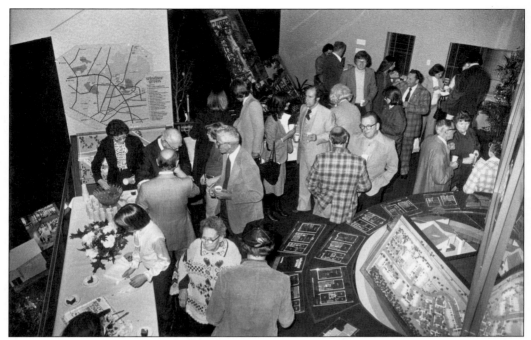

Windsor Green is a community of 654 houses built in 1976. It features a small community center, a large pool, a baby pool, five tennis courts, walking and jogging trails, and playgrounds. Other housing developments in Greenbelt East, as the area is called, include Greenbriar, Greenbrook, Green Springs, and Greenbelt Lake Village. (Courtesy Greenbelt Museum.)

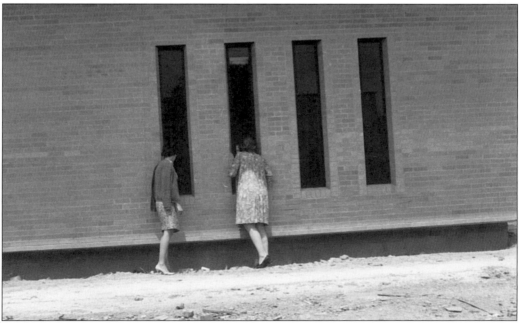

The Greenbelt branch of the Prince George's County Memorial Library system opened in 1970. A ground-breaking event was held in 1968, and curious Greenbelters peered through the windows while the library was under construction in 1969. The library houses a special collection of Greenbelt history–related materials in the Tugwell Room. (Courtesy *Greenbelt News Review*.)

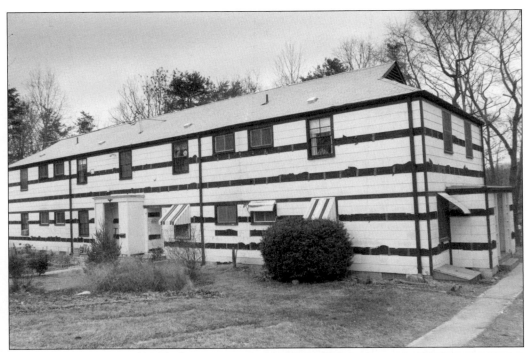

Greenbelt Homes, Inc. (GHI), the housing cooperative that owns and maintains Greenbelt's original housing, has continued to thrive over the years but has also faced challenges. In the late 1970s into the early 1980s, GHI undertook several different improvement projects involving windows, electrical systems, siding, and converting the heating systems from oil to electrical baseboards. (Both, courtesy *Greenbelt News Review*; right, photograph by Jim Henson.)

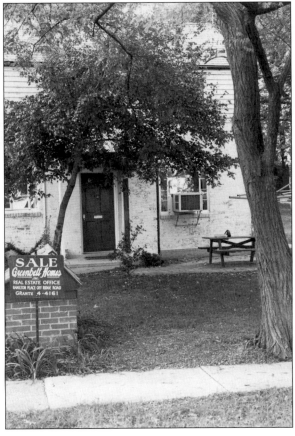

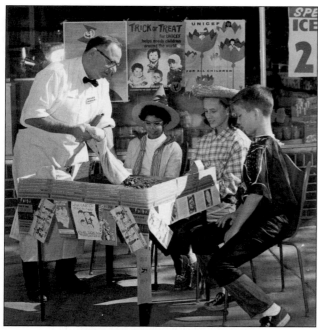

In this photograph, students have set up a table outside of the High's Dairy store in the town center as part of an annual Halloween trick or treat for UNICEF drive. Leo Gerton, then longtime proprietor of the store, assists. He was also well known in town for his annual fish fry at the lake. (Courtesy Greenbelt Museum, photograph by Seymour Kaplan.)

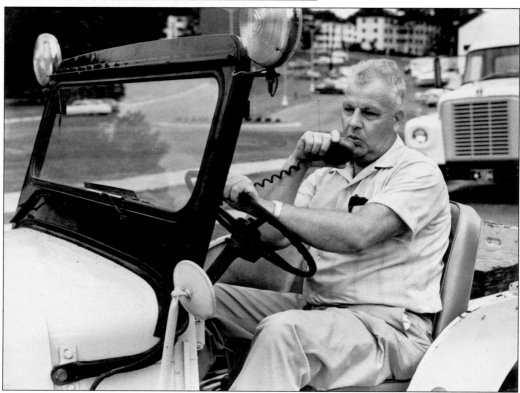

Albert "Buddy" Attick was one of Greenbelt's first police officers and, in the city's early years, was well known for riding his horse throughout the town while on patrol. Later, he became the city's first director of public works, and a City of Greenbelt Jeep became his preferred mode of transport. (Courtesy Greenbelt Museum, photograph by Seymour Kaplan.)

Seven

THE 1980S AND BEYOND

In 1987, Greenbelt reached its 50th year, and with that milestone came the realization that the unique history of the community warranted both celebration and preservation. In 1987, the city celebrated its 50th anniversary with a yearlong series of events, activities, and publications. Other significant events in the 1980s included increased development in Greenbelt East and the opening of Eleanor Roosevelt High School, so named because Greenbelters protested when the school board suggested that it be named for her husband, FDR. In the 1990s, the city undertook a major historical preservation project in restoring and repurposing Center School into a dedicated community center. Despite a controversial start, the community center reopened in 1997 and is now a vital space for the community, containing the following: a gym, an adult day care facility, the *News Review* office, a co-op nursery school, the city planning department, a television studio, the arts division of the recreation department, artist studios, gallery space, exhibit space, museum offices, ceramic studios, and a dark room.

As of 2012, Greenbelt is 75 years old, and over the last 25 years, the city has expanded significantly beyond its original population and grown increasingly diverse. The community has weathered many different periods of growth and has tried to balance development with preservation of the principles on which it was founded. There are many challenges ahead, however, including an aging housing stock, increasing traffic on local highways, and a still-shaky economy. Large federal government entities on Greenbelt's borders help in terms of job stability, as many residents are employed by the federal government at the Beltsville Agricultural Research Center and NASA's Goddard Space Flight Center. Residents are already doing some of the things they do best to respond to these challenges. They are forming committees, organizing, and getting involved. Sustainability, for instance, was the focus of a series of meetings that were part of the Greener Greenbelt Initiative, sponsored by GHI and the Potomac Valley Chapter of the American Institute of Architects in 2007. The newly established farmer's market and the Greenbelt Co-op Supermarket are thriving. Residents recycle, garden, and can even buy wind energy. They serve on official committees such as the Advisory Committee on Trees, the Forest Preserve Advisory Board, and the Advisory Committee on Environmental Sustainability, just to name a few. As the Washington region becomes more and more crowded, Greenbelt's original plan, with its walkable commercial areas, integration of housing and green space, numerous parks and recreation areas, and history of community activism all seem especially inviting. Greenbelt, ahead of its time in 1937, is perhaps finally being recognized as the model community its planners hoped it would be, and the green focus built into its roots will help it survive long into the future.

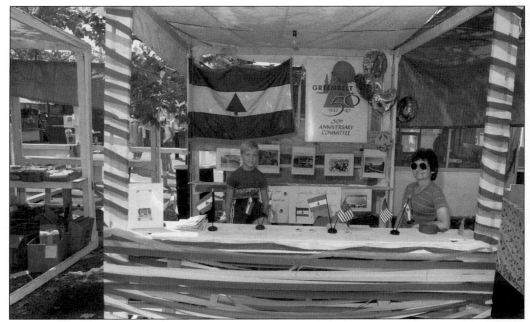

Plans for Greenbelt's 50th anniversary were begun several years earlier by a committee appointed by city council. Sandra (Barnes) Lange, pictured here staffing a booth on Labor Day, chaired the committee. During the yearlong celebration, Greenbelters reflected on the creation of their city, organized events, sponsored a conference for national and international scholars on Greenbelt's legacy, founded and opened the Greenbelt Museum, and wrote and published a milestone book, *Greenbelt: History of a New Town*, edited by Mary Lou Williamson, which is still the primary resource historians use to learn about the city. (Courtesy *Greenbelt News Review.*)

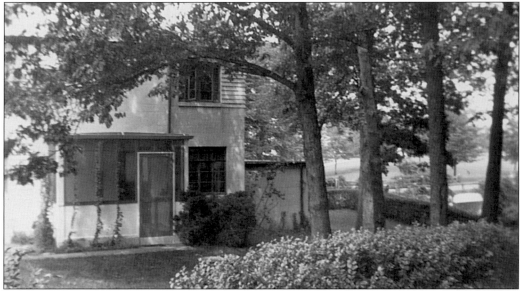

The museum subcommittee of the 50th Anniversary Committee sent letters to selected homeowners in Greenbelt inquiring if they would be interested in selling their home to the city so that a house museum could be created. The owners of 10B Crescent Road were willing, and the work to restore the house to its original appearance began. (Courtesy Greenbelt Museum.)

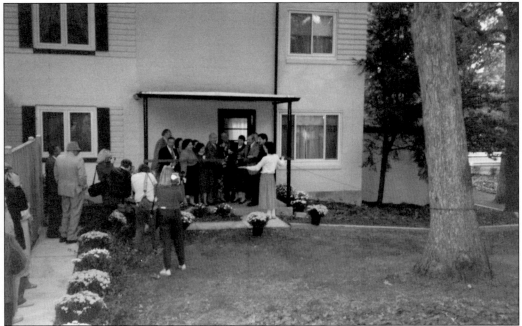

The house at 10B Crescent Road is pictured here post-restoration. The museum opened on October 10, 1987, and was a popular attraction the during the 50th-anniversary homecoming weekend, held from October 9 to 11, 1987. Many of Greenbelt's pioneer families returned to visit, and oral histories were collected and published by one of the museum's founders, Dorothy Lauber, in a volume entitled *Looking Back*. (Courtesy Greenbelt Museum.)

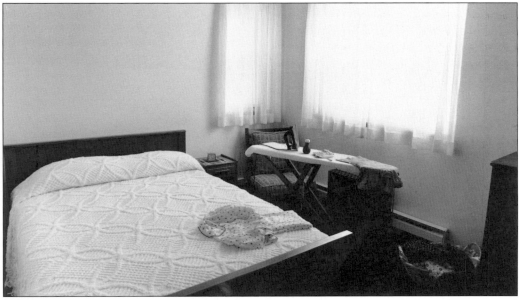

The Greenbelt Museum's historic house is furnished with objects primarily from the 1930s and 1940s that have been donated by Greenbelt pioneer families and city residents. The two-bedroom cinder block unit suggests what life would have been like for a typical Greenbelt family between 1937, when the city opened, and 1952, when it was sold by the federal government. (Courtesy Greenbelt Museum, photograph by Bill Cornett.)

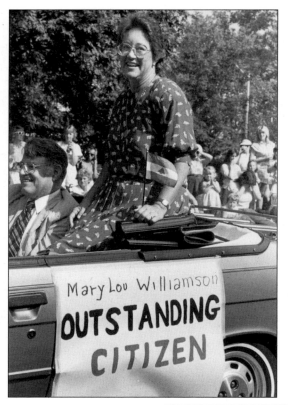

Each year, Greenbelters nominate their fellow residents to be Outstanding Citizen of the Year, and a committee chooses the winner. In 1985, the committee chose Mary Lou Williamson for her years of work on the *Greenbelt News Review*, the city's independent newspaper. The newspaper has been one of the most important elements in the development of Greenbelt's identity, as it has allowed residents to share important information quickly and has fostered the community's legacy of activism. (Courtesy *Greenbelt News Review*.)

James K. Giese was another recipient of the outstanding citizen award (in 2010). He was Greenbelt's city manager from 1962 to 1991 and, in conjunction with city council and active citizens, was able to guide the city smoothly through a period of rapid growth and development. He has volunteered for many years with the *News Review*, the Greenbelt Museum, and many other organizations and committees. (Courtesy Greenbelt Museum, photograph by Renee Bryan.)

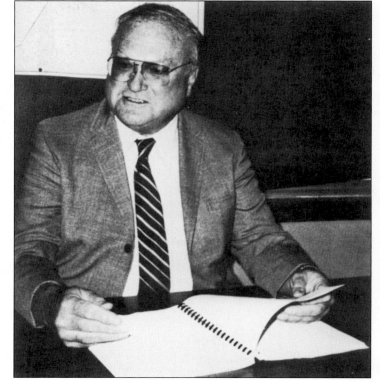

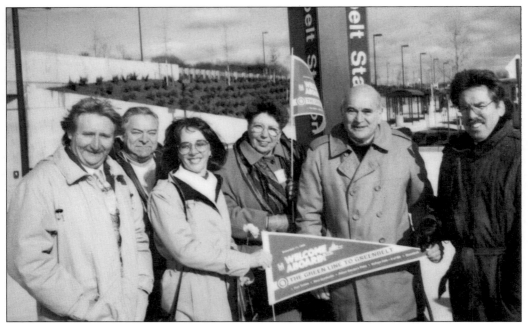

After many years of construction, the Washington, DC, region's Metro system finally opened the Green Line to Greenbelt in 1993. In this photograph, members of the city council hold a "welcome aboard" pennant. From left to right are Rodney Roberts, Lester Whitmer, Judith Davis, Antoinette Bram, Mayor Gil Weidenfeld, and city manager Daniel Hobbs. Below, Metro riders study a map of the area on opening day of the Greenbelt station. (Both, courtesy *Greenbelt News Review*.)

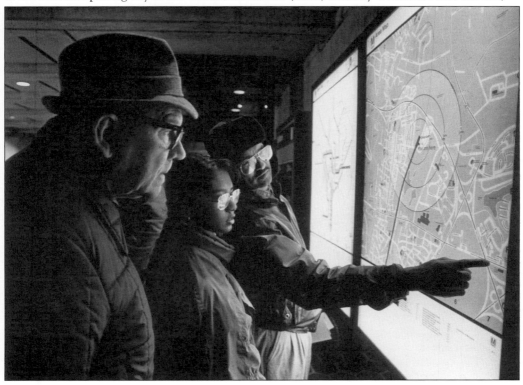

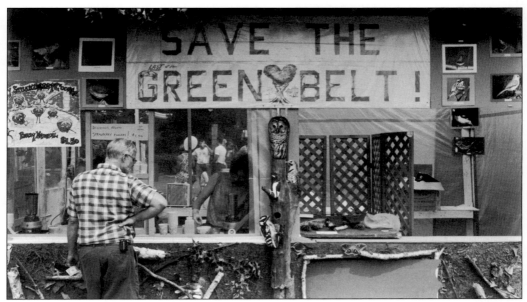

Save the Greenbelt is an organization formed by citizens to preserve the remaining green space that once encircled the city. Originally intended to be an intact buffer against encroaching development and a site for farming and recreation, Greenbelt's actual green belt has been depleted over the years. The residential and commercial development and expansion, however, has allowed the city to grow to nearly 23,000 people since its beginning, and both the city government and GHI still preserve portions of the green belt. (Courtesy *Greenbelt News Review*.)

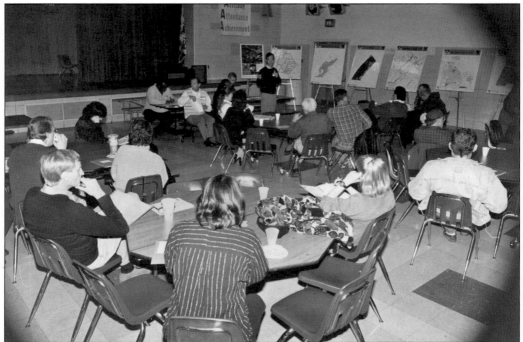

Greenbelt residents continue to organize meetings to discuss issues. In this photograph, concerned Greenbelters gather in 1997 to discuss development plans for the area around the Greenbelt Metro station. (Courtesy *Greenbelt News Review*, photograph by Prospero Zevallos.)

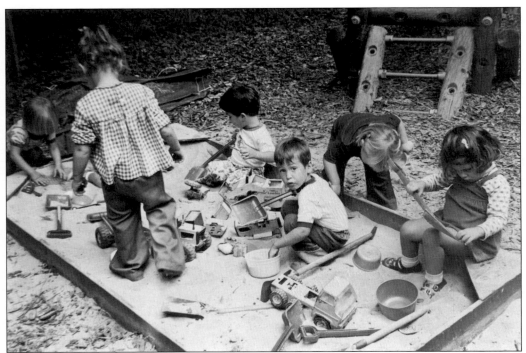

Greenbelt Co-op Nursery School was opened in April 1941. Early resident David Granahan recalled, "A nursery school was started by a group of young mothers for their three and four year olds and a teacher was hired. The mothers took turns helping in the classroom and the playground and the fathers got together and constructed sturdy toys for the children." Today, parents with children at the nursery school must participate in the cooperative, and many work shifts there each week. At right, nursery school students in the early 1980s hold a sign asking residents to refrain from littering. (Both, courtesy *Greenbelt News Review*.)

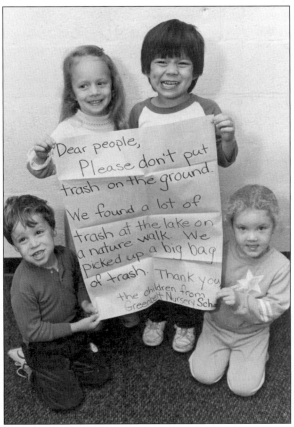

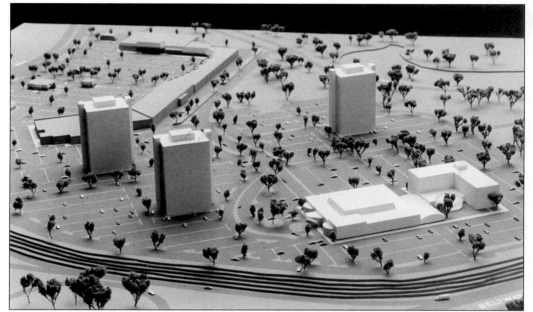

Greenbelt East witnessed increased development in the 1980s and 1990s. This model depicts the Greenway Shopping Center and Maryland Trade Center buildings. Greenway Center opened in 1980, featuring what was at the time the largest Safeway store on the east coast. The trade center buildings opened throughout the decade. (Courtesy *Greenbelt News Review*, photograph by Ed Barnette.)

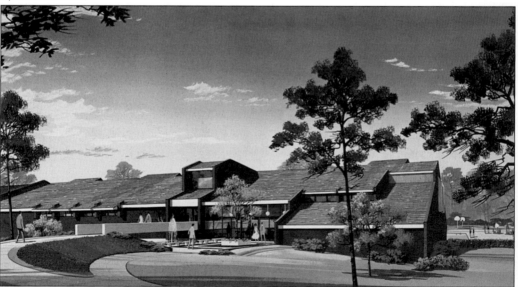

Greenbriar is a large housing development in Greenbelt East, an area of the city that continued to grow in the 1980s. It was built by developer Alan Kay between 1974 and 1980, despite opposition from Greenbelt citizens who were members of the Save Our Community Committee. According to marketing materials produced at the time, it featured "health clubs, sauna baths, card rooms, billiard rooms, table tennis rooms, and meeting rooms," all in addition to outdoor recreational facilities such as tennis courts, pools, shuffleboard, and children's playgrounds. (Courtesy Tugwell Room, Greenbelt branch of Prince George's County Memorial Library.)

116

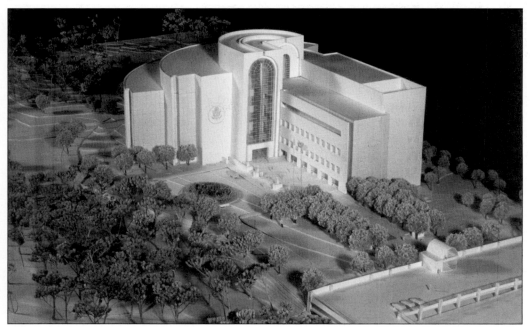

Construction of the US District Court for the District of Maryland, shown above in model form, began in Greenbelt in October 1991. Since 1996, the courthouse has hosted an art program with changing exhibitions featuring everything from local to international art. (Courtesy *Greenbelt News Review*.)

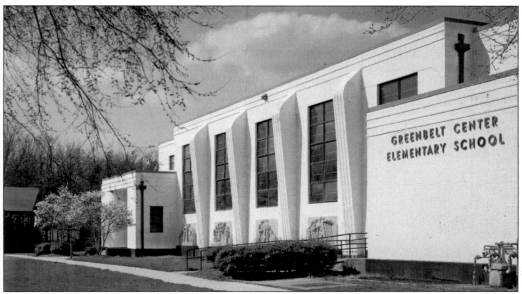

Center School had been transferred to the Prince George's County Board of Education in the late 1950s, but by the late 1980s, the building no longer served the county's needs. Greenbelt citizens and historic preservationists fought to save the building and turn it into a community center, though the community was deeply divided on the issue. In the end, the land originally occupied by the North End Elementary School was traded, and the county built a new elementary school there. (Courtesy Greenbelt Museum, photograph by Jack Boucher for the Historic American Buildings Survey.)

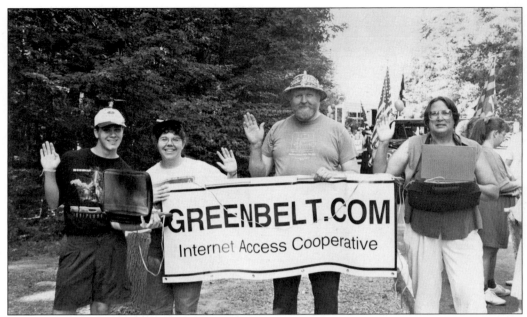

The cooperative spirit entered the digital age in Greenbelt when the Greenbelt Internet Access Cooperative was formed in 1996. According to its website, the organization is "a non-stock Maryland cooperative organized and operated by community volunteers to help others learn about and access the Internet. GIAC also offers Internet access, e-mail, website hosting, and other services to its members via greenbelt.com." (Courtesy *Greenbelt News Review*.)

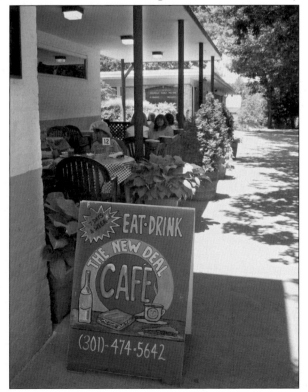

On December 30, 1995, the New Deal Café opened for limited hours in the Greenbelt Community Center. Operated by an all-volunteer staff and funded by member donations, it provided patrons with a place to meet, drink, and eat. By 2000, the café had moved to Roosevelt Center. In addition to serving food, the New Deal has also become a venue for art exhibits and live music and is run as a cooperative. (Courtesy Greenbelt Museum, photograph by Megan Searing Young.)

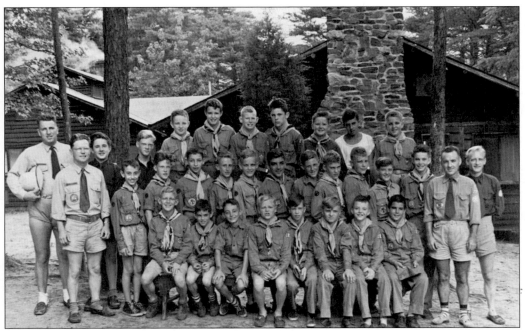

Greenbelt's youth have long participated in Boy Scouts, Girl Scouts, and Camp Fire organizations. Pictured here are the Greenbelt Boy Scout troop at Camp Roosevelt in Chesapeake Beach, Maryland, in 1950 and the Greenbelt Girl Scouts marching in the Labor Day parade. (Above, courtesy Lee Shields; below, courtesy Greenbelt Museum, photograph by Paul Kasko.)

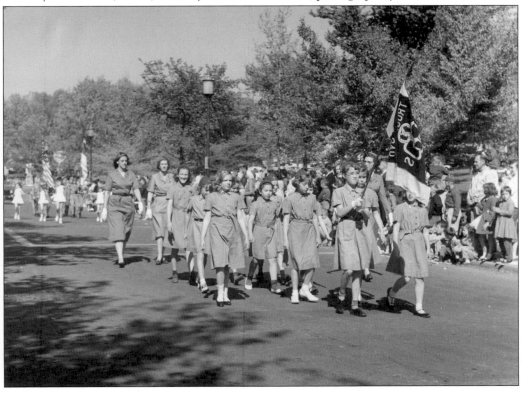

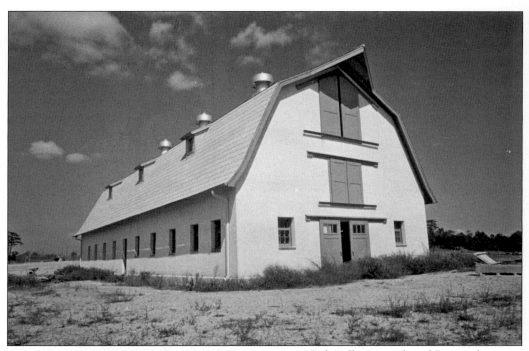

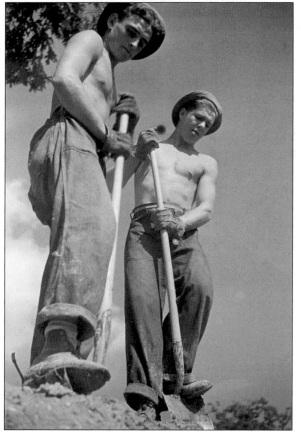

Beltsville Agricultural Research Center (BARC) was established in 1935 by Henry Wallace, secretary of agriculture. The Civilian Conservation Corps was used to build many of the early buildings on the site, as pictured above. According to its website, "BARC is the largest and most diversified agricultural research complex in the world." It conducts research in animal health, human nutrition, maintaining America's agricultural economy, and food safety. BARC employs over 8,000 people and conducts 1,200 research projects. It abuts Greenbelt's northern border and provides a green buffer for the community. (Both, courtesy Library of Congress.)

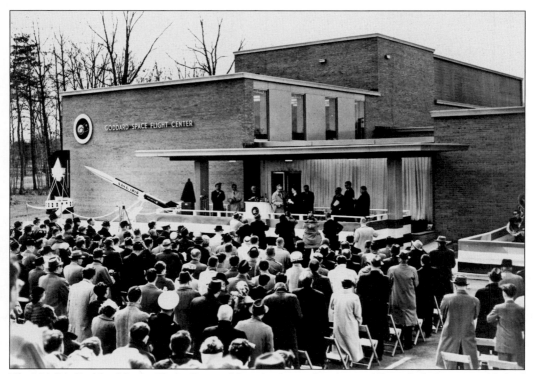

The NASA Goddard Space Flight Center (above) is located just east of Greenbelt. It was established May 1, 1959, and dedicated on March 16, 1961. The center has employed many Greenbelt residents over the years and continues to do so. Initially called the Beltsville Space Flight Center, it was eventually named for Dr. Robert H. Goddard, a pioneer in rocketry. The land on which the space flight center was built was originally part of the Beltsville Agriculture Research Center. In 1987, the space flight center helped Greenbelt celebrate its 50th anniversary (below). (Above, courtesy NASA; below, courtesy Greenbelt Museum.)

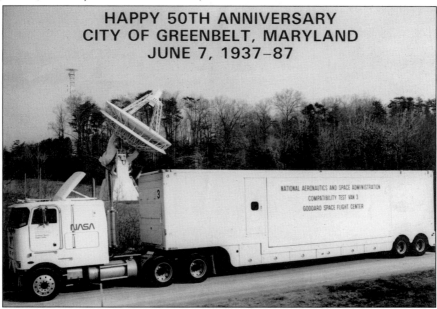

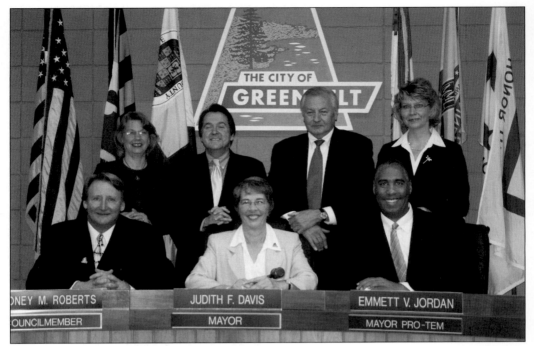

Pictured here are the current members of the city council of Greenbelt, as of 2009. From left to right are Rodney Roberts, Leta Mach, Konrad Herling, Mayor Judith Davis, Edward Putens, Mayor Pro Tem Emmett Jordan, and Silke Pope. (Courtesy City of Greenbelt.)

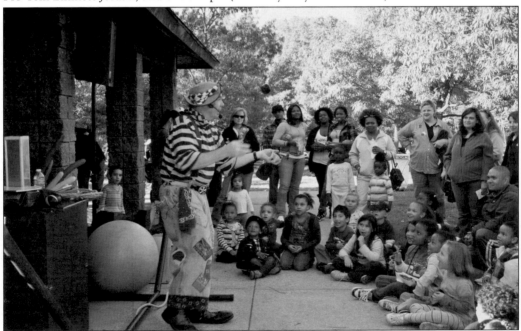

Schrom Hills Park is another of the city's recreational areas. Located in Greenbelt East, the park is host to Fall Fest each year, and residents of all ages come to enjoy performances, activities, and the change of seasons. Greg May clowns for a group of children at the festival. (Courtesy City of Greenbelt, photograph by Beverly Palau.)

The Greenbelt Farmer's Market, established in 2008 and run by local residents, attracts community members concerned about both eating locally and the sustainability of local farms. The market operates from May to November and only allows vendors who reside within a 100-mile radius or are within the state of Maryland. (Courtesy Greenbelt Museum.)

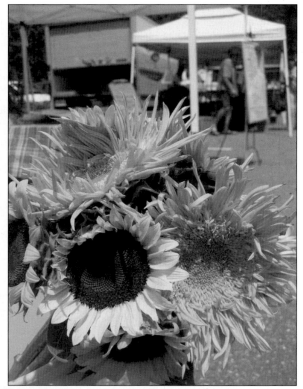

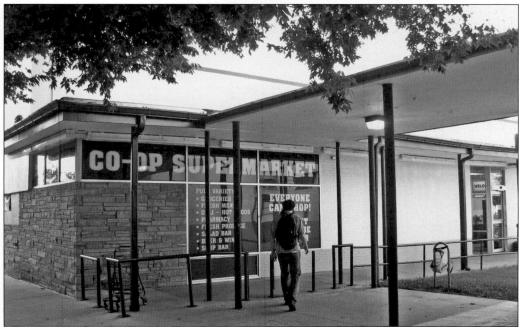

The Greenbelt Co-op Supermarket and Pharmacy, still located in historic Greenbelt in what is now called Roosevelt Center, continues to thrive. It is owned by its more than 6,000 local members, though consumers do not have to be members to shop there. (Courtesy Greenbelt Museum, photograph by Megan Searing Young.)

123

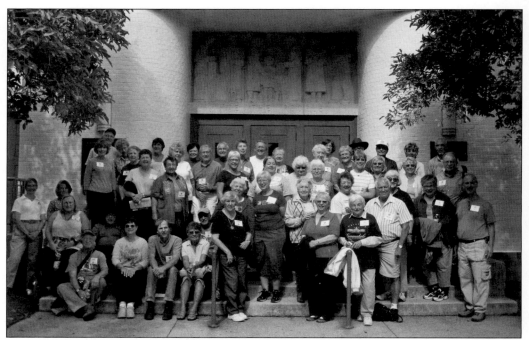

In 2010, a group of residents from Greendale, one of Greenbelt's sister cities, travelled by bus to visit the city. They toured the historic section of town and mingled with Greenbelt residents at a luncheon cosponsored by the City of Greenbelt and the Friends of the Greenbelt Museum. (Courtesy Greenbelt Museum.)

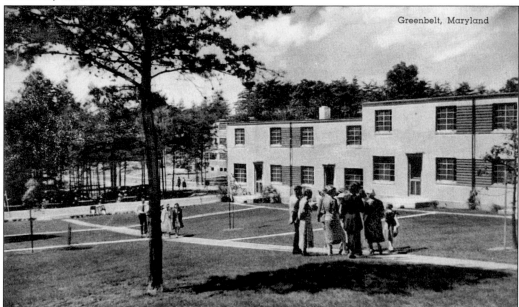

When Greenbelt opened in 1937, it was a tourist attraction, as seen in this c. 1938 postcard. Early residents report having visitors peek into their windows and stop them to ask what life was like in the planned community. Greenbelt continues to attract local, national, and international visitors, and the Greenbelt Museum regularly gives tours to visitors from Japan, Germany, Australia, and the United Kingdom. (Courtesy Greenbelt Museum.)

In 2010, the Greenbelt Museum installed a temporary exhibition entitled *Green from the Start: A History of Gardening in Greenbelt* to explore and celebrate the many ways in which Greenbelt was designed with sustainability in mind, long before being green was popular. Joe Parisi designed this poster for the museum by adapting an original victory garden poster by WPA artist Hubert Morley and incorporating artwork by Dan Kennedy. Many educational programs have accompanied the exhibit, including a seed exchange, as depicted below. The head of the Greenbelt Garden Club for many years, John Henry Jones, exchanges a seed packet with Barbara Havekost, one of the museum's founders and a longtime museum volunteer. (Both, courtesy Greenbelt Museum.)

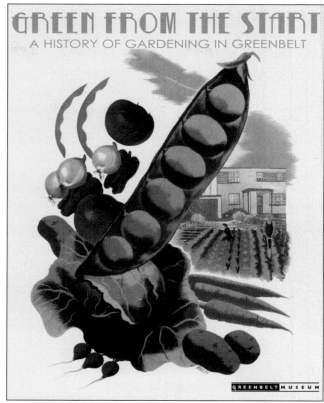

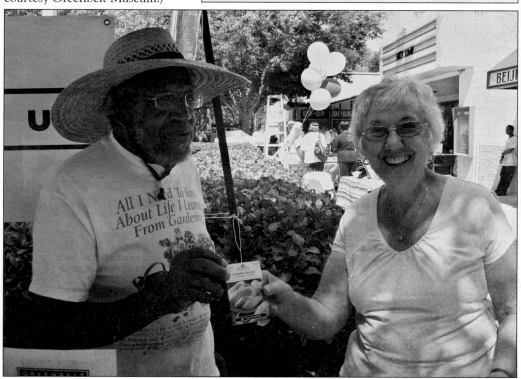

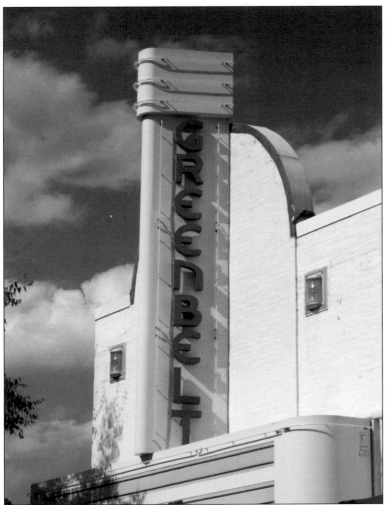

The City of Greenbelt restored the movie theater marquee to its streamlined splendor in 2000, and in 2002, the city purchased the building. It boasts a 40-foot cinemascope screen, a Dolby digital sound system, and 500 seats. It remains one of the only single-screen theaters in the area. (Courtesy Greenbelt Museum, photograph by Megan Searing Young.)

Many of Greenbelt's beloved traditions continue, like the annual Fourth of July celebration at the lake, complete with fireworks. In this photograph, Thomas Cherrix leads the 40-member Greenbelt Concert Band. (Courtesy *Greenbelt News Review*, photograph by Prospero Zevallos.)

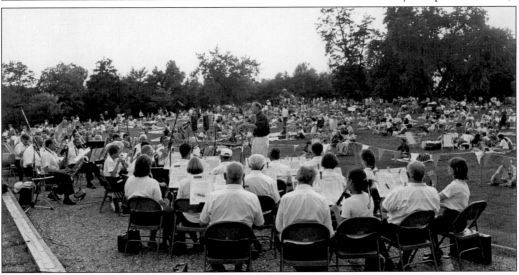

BIBLIOGRAPHY

"American Housing: A Failure, A Problem, A Potential Boon and Boom." *Life* magazine (November 1937): 45.

Arnold, Joseph. *The New Deal in the Suburbs; A History of the Greenbelt Town Program, 1935–1954.* Columbus: Ohio State University Press, 1971.

Farm Security Administration/City of Greenbelt. *Greenbelt Maryland Manual.* Greenbelt, MD, 1942.

Fulmer, Otis Kline. *Greenbelt.* Washington, DC: American Council on Public Affairs, 1941.

Klaus, Susan L. *Links in the Chain: Greenbelt, Maryland and the New Town Movement in America: An Annotated Bibliography on the Occasion of the Fiftieth Anniversary of Greenbelt, Maryland.* Washington, DC: Center for Washington Area Studies, George Washington University, 1987.

Knepper, Cathy. *Greenbelt, Maryland: A Living Legacy of the New Deal.* Baltimore: Johns Hopkins University Press, 2001.

Lauber, Dorothy, ed. *Looking Back: A Collection of Recollections of Greenbelt Residents and Others.* Greenbelt, MD: City of Greenbelt 1982.

Resettlement Administration. *Greenbelt Towns.* Washington, DC: US Government, 1936.

Stein, Clarence S. *Toward New Towns for America.* Cambridge, MA: MIT Press, 1957; rev. ed., 1969.

Warner, George A. *Greenbelt: The Cooperative Community, An Experience in Democratic Living.* New York: Exposition Press, 1954.

Williamson, Mary Lou, ed. *Greenbelt: History of a New Town, 1937–1987.* Norfolk, VA: Donning Company Publishers, 1987.

www.arcadiapublishing.com

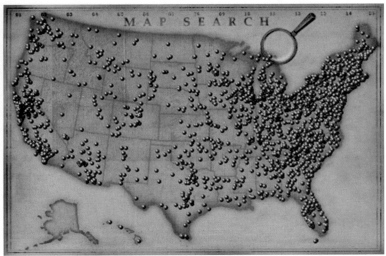

Discover books about the town where you grew up, the cities where your friends and families live, the town where your parents met, or even that retirement spot you've been dreaming about. Our Web site provides history lovers with exclusive deals, advanced notification about new titles, e-mail alerts of author events, and much more.

 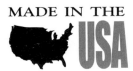
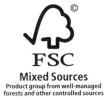
Find Your Place in History.